Consumer Driven Health Care

by
Roger D. Blackwell, Ph.D. &
Thomas E. Williams, M.D., Ph.D.
Alan A. Ayers, MBA, MAcc

Copyright ©2005, Book Publishing Associates, Inc.

ISBN 0-9767449-0-2

LCCN 2005902030

Printed in the United States of America

Contents

ACKNOWLEDGEMENTS
v

CHAPTER 1
*How to Avoid Drowning in
a Flood of Health Care Costs*
1

CHAPTER 2
Is Your Job Next to Go?
17

CHAPTER 3
Global Thinking About Health Care
33

CHAPTER 4
The Crisis of Indirect Health Care Costs
57

CHAPTER 5
The Crisis of the Direct Costs of Health Care
83

CHAPTER 6
The Inevitable Polarity of Health Care Delivery
101

CHAPTER 7
*How a Health Savings Account
Fights the Evils of First Dollar Coverage*
121

CHAPTER 8
More Health Care Is Not the Answer
139

CHAPTER 9
Obesity and the "Miracle Cure"
151

CHAPTER 10
Who Will Solve the Problem?
169

APPENDIX
*Modern Achievements in
Medicine and Public Health*
183

ABOUT THE AUTHORS
187

INDEX
189

Foreword

Amerika is all about people who want something better—for themselves, their families, and their communities. There is no greater example of this than our expectations for medical care both in sickness and in health. For patients, something better usually means relief from pain or disease and freedom to live the life they'd experienced before they were ill; to again dream for the future. For physicians, something better usually means freedom to pursue a noble profession, treat their patients without burdensome bureaucracy and inefficiency, and be a respected part of their community. For the staff and boards of health care institutions, something better usually means an expectation that their particular institution will deliver the highest standards of care; be sensitive to the needs, feelings, and abilities of those they serve; and always be there on a moment's notice with the right answers and the right people. For policy makers, both in government and private industry, who together assume the financial responsibilities for the majority of care through taxes and payroll respectively, the cost of all this dominates their thinking and all too often deflects attention from the essence of medicine—care of patients one by one. That is, the individual consumer. Increasingly it's money that's on their minds.

To each of these groups achieving better can only be accomplished if they all make an effort to grasp the broader policy issues and management choices that feed into each of their individual objectives. Each shares with the other the common goal of better health and well-being for all Americans, and that becomes the vehicle of communication and understanding upon which solutions to seemingly at-odds objectives will come.

In my own professional life, I have cared for patients, led medical and research institutions, and served in government. The overriding realities of my life in medicine are that the extraordinary advances in technology and science have brought a continuous stream of technologies and know-how to cure disease, maintain health, and improve quality of life. And because of sustained investment in medical research and technology and its translation into tomorrow's medicine, we have hope for virtually all of the nagging diseases that still outsmart us. Whether it be the many degenerative brain diseases, or cancer, diabetes, or heart failure, we see daily advances. Why is it then that we cannot make similar progress in the process of administering the institutions and vast resources that deliver health care to each consumer, and which ultimately drive the scientific breakthroughs? Can we accomplish these goals at a cost that makes the benefits we're capable of delivering available to the widest possible populations of the society we serve today and tomorrow? Or is this riddle unsolvable?

To help answer these questions are Dr. Roger Blackwell and Dr. Tom Williams. In this thought-provoking book based upon the unique backgrounds of two researchers, each with more than 40 years of experience in their respective areas, these two doctors analyze how institutions evolve in response to a changing economic environment and patient care. Dr. Williams's passion for patients is well known in both his specialized area of surgery as well as his service in emerging nations in remote parts of the globe. A passion for understanding consumer behavior and its role in creating customer-centric organizations led Dr. Blackwell to write the first text on consumer behavior, now translated into many languages and used in nations around the world. Together, these two men bring a unique set of skills to analyzing the problem of how the U.S. health care system is changing to become more patient-centric and economically affordable. If it doesn't, as they describe in Chapter 2, the jobs of ordinary Americans will be directly threatened and the delivery of effective health care will be increasingly questioned.

Drs. Blackwell and Williams describe the problems that have developed as third-party payers, not users of the health care system, evolved to the point of paying routine, expected costs of health care. Now, the pendulum is swinging back to a system in which consumers are forced to retake control of much of their own health care expenditures, not by choice but by necessity, as well as control of their own personal health. The authors' thesis is that this trend will lead to a more efficient system that will again make health care accessible and affordable for those who need it most.

For health care institutions, administrators, and policy makers, the transition from a third-party payer system to a consumer driven health care system, although painful for some participants, is inevitable—as inevitable as the institutional life cycle the authors describe among airlines, banks, and department stores in Chapter 6. Medicine today is complex, high-tech, and expensive and without innovations and efficiency borrowed from other economic sectors, the United States won't have the funds to research, develop, and implement a health care system that already absorbs more than 15 percent of the nation's resources, making it a national $2 trillion crisis.

Research and medical practice advances have made possible everyday medical "miracles," but at enormous costs. These are not only economic costs but also the costs of making insurance companies, instead of patients, the customers, creating a wedge in the inviolable relationship between caregiver and patient. The authors suggest the next "miracle" will be driven by consumers, both the miracle that creates better health and the miracle that creates a more responsive, efficient health care system. But this will only happen if consumers themselves step up to the task, thinking personally, but also long term for themselves and their children.

It's a provocative book, one that can be read in a relatively few hours, but when absorbed is likely to produce a dialogue and changes that will last for years.

Bernadine Healy, M.D.

Bernadine Healy, M.D. is a cardiologist and health administrator known for direct communication, innovative policymaking, and forward looking leadership in medical and research institutions. Currently Dr. Healy is Medical and Health Columnist for *U.S. News and World Report* and serves on the President's Council of Advisors on Science and Technology. Previously she led the Research Institute at the Cleveland Clinic, the National Institutes of Health, the College of Medicine and Public Health at the Ohio State University, the American Heart Association, and the American Red Cross.

Acknowledgements

"It takes a village" to write a book of this nature. We are very fortunate to be part of such a village of concerned people who encouraged, contributed to and commented on our efforts to conceptualize what has happened to health care in the United States, the new directions that are clearly (and sometimes painfully) emerging, and where we believe it will go in the future.

Our goal of a comprehensive, easy-to-understand summary of America's health care funding crisis could not have been achieved without the views, assistance, insights and prior research of highly respected colleagues in economics, business, public policy, and medicine. In many instances, some of the theory and concepts are traceable directly to our own professors and courses while studying in Ph.D. programs at Northwestern University.

We gratefully express appreciation to the late Dr. Wayne Talarzyk, chairman of the marketing department at The Ohio State University, co-author of *Consumer Attitudes Toward Health Care and Medical Malpractice* and contributor to many of the concepts in the first four chapters of this book. Taken much too early by cancer, Wayne's careful analysis and more importantly, his faith, continue to serve as an inspiration to his many students, colleagues and friends.

Special thanks also go to Dr. Leona W. Ayers, professor of pathology at The Ohio State University, who spent countless hours reading, commenting and improving each of the chapters. Much of the credit for what we have written about public health and preventive medicine, especially in Chapter 8, should go to Dr. Ayers.

We are very fortunate to be in a community of scholars called The Ohio State University. One of those scholars and a major contributor to medical research is our President, Dr. Karen Holbrook. Dr. Joe Alutto, dean of the Fisher College of Business is another one of those rare administrators who not only challenges his faculty to achieve excellence in research and teaching, but facilitates it as well. We are deeply appreciative of Dr. Bernadine Healy's leadership in health care and education over many years and her willingness to so freely share her wisdom.

We also want to express appreciation to Margie Williams, a vital member of our team, for contributing encouragement, vision and sometimes chauffeur services, Mary Hiser of Roger Blackwell Associates, Inc., for managing the deluge of email messages between the authors and coordinating their schedules, and the excellent staff of BookMasters for their skillful and rapid assistance of bringing this book to you, our readers.

It is difficult to mention everyone who has made special contributions without including a list that would require many pages. Some of the people listed below helped us by suggesting ideas and research materials. Some read specific chapters and provided broad feedback while others reviewed every chapter with detailed page-by-page comments. We are deeply grateful to each, although we acknowledge that we didn't always do what they suggested and do not want to ascribe their concurrence with everything we describe in the following pages. And in spite of their support, we know that we didn't get it right in every instance and any errors or omissions are the responsibility of the authors, not of those people who helped us in so many ways.

Roger Blackwell
Tom Williams
Alan Ayers

Gratefully, we acknowledge the assistance of the following people:

David Bickelhaupt, Ph.D.
Ann Blackwell
Neeli Bendapudi, Ph.D.
W. C. Benton, Ph.D.
Dick Briggs, M.D.
Steven Burgess, Ph.D.
Dave Carlin
Cindy Collier, Ph.D.
Allen Damschoeder, M.D.
Jack Edwards

Chris Ellison, M.D.
Matt Everard, M.D.
Henry Fabian, M.D.
Karen Fox
Reed Fraley
John Goff, M.D.
Leslie Golan
Josh Harris
Stephen Hills, Ph.D.
Kelley Hughes

Mario LaCute
Ted Jones, M.D.
Michelle Keith
Gladstone McDowell, M.D.
Bob Mack, M.D.
John Makley, M.D.
Catharina Maulbecker-
  Armstrong, Ph.D.
Gerald Medlin
Robert Meier
Rob Michler, M.D.

John Mulligan
Matt Pettinelli
Diane Reynolds
Dan Roberts
David Rubadue
John Rumberger, M.D.
Fred Sanfillipo, M.D., Ph.D.
Scott Semerar
Joy Tutela
Jeff Wilkins
Kathryn R. Wion

—and the thousands of students, patients, colleagues and friends who have shaped our careers and lives over many years.

CHAPTER 1

How to Avoid Drowning in a Flood of Health Care Costs

"Predicting rain doesn't count; building arks does."
—The Noah Principle

A middle-class family with two children, a home mortgage, two automobiles, and a deck of credit cards sits down at the end of the month to balance its budget and notices, despite last year's pay raises, new child tax credits and a lower tax bracket, there is still not enough money to make ends meet. Sure they're still doing better than their neighbors, especially the one across the street who was laid off a few months ago when his software engineering job was "outsourced" to India, but the family still asks, "Where is it all going?" After careful examination, the family discovers higher payroll deductions for employee health insurance, payroll taxes for Medicare, and higher out-of-pocket expenses including co-pays for physician visits and pharmaceuticals. "Something has got to be done," the family proclaims, "but certainly socialized medicine is not the answer."

As this family came to realize, America's rising health care costs are attacking the livelihood and well-being of its people. In 2004, U.S. health care expenditures hit $1.7 trillion, consuming 15.3 percent of the total output of goods and services—greater than any other industrialized country. If allowed to continue, the total will reach $2 trillion in the next couple of years, making it even more difficult for the United States to compete in a global economy. Meanwhile, the personal health of Americans continues to deteriorate with lifestyle-induced illnesses challenging many of the gains in longevity achieved by medical science.

All Americans should ask themselves the troubling question, "Will I be able to afford the quality of health care that I need to achieve and maintain good health leading to a long life?" Even if the answer is yes, "Will my children and grandchildren be able to afford it?" Or, will we be driven to some sort of overburdened system—rationing or maybe even a lottery—to decide who gets the care they need and, by default, who does not?

Every physician and health care provider must also ask the question, "Will I be able to use the latest, most effective technology to treat patients?" Or, "Before I see a new patient, will I have to determine which diagnoses and treatments are allowed and reimbursed by that patient's insurance policy?"

Every employer faces the business question, "Should I continue to employ Americans in my business with health care costs twice those of other industrialized nations?" Or, "Should I simply outsource as many jobs as possible to countries where health care costs are much less?" And governments must decide whether to levy even higher taxes, reduce benefits on existing entitlements, or divert funds from other vital services such as education, transportation, and public safety.

It's time for change which, whether recognized or not, is already occurring as American consumers—people like you—begin to understand what is at stake and make decisions that improve the quality and efficiency of the health care system while taking responsibility for their own personal health. This book is about that process, which we call consumer driven health care.

The Problem of Rising Health Care Costs

When you look at the upward trend in health care costs and conservative projections for the future, the adverse effect on economic growth is alarming. As illustrated by Exhibits 1.1 and 1.2, national health care spending is expected to continue rising from its present level of about $6,000 per person to more than $9,000 by 2010. Moreover, the percentage of Gross Domestic Product (GDP) consumed by health care will rise from 15 percent to nearly 18 percent. In practical terms that means nearly one out of every five dollars in goods and services produced in the United States will be diverted to health care!

The debate over rising health care costs encompasses such economically dire consequences that the most important questions often go unasked. For example, "When someone is ill, how much should be spent to help him get well?" For the most part, America's collective answer has been, "Whatever it takes." Yet, when 45 million Amer-

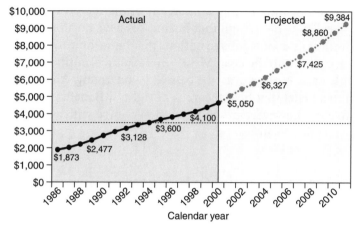

Exhibit 1.1   National Health Expenditures Per Capita, 1986–2010

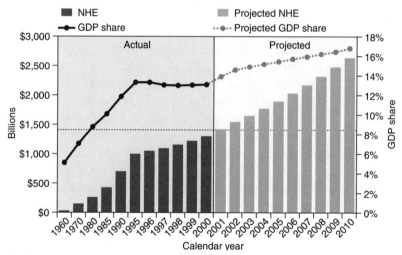

Exhibit 1.2   National Health Expenditures and Their Share of Gross Domestic Product (GDP), 1960–2010

icans are uninsured and data clearly indicate that "whatever it takes" may be more than anyone (or everyone) can afford, some conclude it is "someone else's" responsibility to pay.

Until recently "someone else" was employer-sponsored health insurance, or for older and underprivileged Americans, the federal government. Regardless of how the funds are raised, the decision to spend more on health care necessarily requires spending less on other things.

Even if we are willing to pay 20 percent of the nation's GDP, "whatever it takes" may be so high that businesses have no alternative but to limit coverage or export jobs to nations that know how to provide quality health care at half the cost. Most Americans feel entitled to first-dollar health care coverage as a "benefit" and many Americans have evolved to a belief that health care is a "right." "Benefits" and "rights" in health care, however, are on a collision course with a limited number of available resources.

Profits Are as Essential to Business as Breathing Is to People

When the stock market soared from 1999 to 2001 in what Alan Greenspan described as "irrational exuberance," investors started to believe that speed-to-market, market share and other factors were more indicative of a company's success than profits. Investors then learned the hard lesson that sages such as Warren Buffet have long understood, namely that stocks have no value in companies that have no profits. When the stock market "bubble" burst, millions of Americans' "401(k)s" became "201(k)s" as it turned out the "new economy" was nothing new at all. The same economic principles that have always worked still mandate that the firms with the greatest profits, achieved by better marketing, greater innovation, higher quality, or lower costs, will be most successful in the global marketplace. Profits may not be the sole reason businesses exist, but they are required for any business to survive. Or, as the world's most influential business writer, Peter Drucker, once observed for organizations, that profits are as "essential as breathing."

If you were a fly on the wall of corporate board rooms in recent years, you would have observed an amazing transformation as firms struggled to survive in a changing marketplace. Management cut costs and improved productivity in every area, except one—the cost of health care. In board meeting after board meeting, directors looked at the line on profit and loss statements labeled "employee benefits," furled their brows, lowered their faces and simply confessed, "We don't know what else we can do; health care costs just keep going up at double digit rates!"

Firms cannot continue to stay in business if forced to absorb the skyrocketing costs of health care. In governmental and nonprofit organizations, soaring employee benefits costs may result in higher taxes or fewer services provided. Firms expected to turn a profit, however, have little choice but to reduce the number of employees or cut wages. That's why, as we describe in Chapter 2, unless the problem is solved quickly, your job may be the next one to go. And it's why employees now feel the effect of rising health care costs through higher payroll deductions for health insurance, greater restrictions on care, and rising co-pays when they visit a physician or pharmacy.

Looking for an easy answer, some consumers might say, "The government should pay." While superficially appealing, that solution actually adds to health care costs. The government is "us," and has no money except what it takes from American consumers (in the form of taxes) and then pays back to health care providers, at a multiple of the original costs to cover massive bureaucratic and administrative expenses. When taxes are levied on businesses that have no money except what they receive from customers, there is no alternative except to raise the prices charged to consumers. Either way, consumers pay. It's the equivalent of saying, "I will pay my health care costs by imposing taxes on me, sending the money to the government—at either the state or federal level—having the government add the costs of administering the system and then pay the higher costs for me."

The only way to lower health care costs is to lower the costs of operating the system. The current health care system controlled by third-party payers is inherently inefficient, diverting large sums of money from treatment and prevention of illness to bureaucracy and paperwork. When the "buyer" of health care is an employer, insurance company, or the government, the actual users of health care (consumers) are shortchanged as they lack the economic power to influence health care providers.

Can you imagine a consumer going into a retailer and being told, "In order to make a profit, we're going to give you the poorest quality service at the highest possible price?" Certainly such a store wouldn't be in business for long! Yet in health care, consumers become "expenses" that third-party payers work to reduce or even eliminate, rather than "revenue" to be captured. Moreover, when a third-party pays all the bills, there is little incentive for consumers to make choices that reduce overall health care costs—the greatest choice being to "get and stay healthy." Consumer driven health care represents a shift from third parties controlling health care by deciding what's best for large groups of people, to consumers taking control of their own personal health.

Does the United States Have a Health Care System?

Before a solution can be found to America's "Two Trillion Dollar Crisis," the question must be asked, "Does the United States have a health care system?" Examined objectively, the conclusion should be that it does not, at least not a very good one, but it does have a well-developed and very expensive "sickness care" system.

Remarkable advances in the treatment of heart disease, cancer and other maladies have become so expected that the TV program "E.R." and newspaper and magazine articles have persuaded Americans that medical miracles are a reasonable expectation for nearly every condition. Perhaps it's a blockbuster drug or innovative surgical procedure that if not available now, is just around the corner. We've come to expect the system to flawlessly resolve the most serious of traumas while soothing everyday aches and pains. While faith in medical science provides life-sustaining hope for people who are already ill, it's not a particularly good safety net for consumers who neglect their own personal health.

Despite a world-class "sickness care" system, relatively little money, professional knowledge, and consumer interest is directed towards promoting and achieving health. You'll read in Chapter 8 that each year the United States spends thousands of dollars per person on "curative medicine," but less than a couple of dollars on "preventive medicine."

The Four Components of a Health Care System

A nation's health care system consists of four major components: technology, economics, lifestyles and culture, and legal and political processes (including governmental funding and regulation). As illustrated in Exhibit 1.3, each is a major factor in determining not only the *health* of a nation, but also the *cost* of health care.

Technology

No area of science is advancing more rapidly than our understanding of the human body. What Leonardo da Vinci discovered by care-

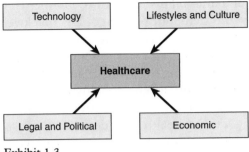

Exhibit 1.3

fully dissecting cadavers, is now probed with magnetic resonance imaging (MRI), microsurgery, invasive radiology and molecular pathology. Increasingly, rapid advances in health care involve inter-disciplinary applications in chemistry, electrical engineering, physics, biology, physiology, psychology, sociology and just about every other "ology" that can be imagined. Technology provides the potential for satisfying consumer health care needs with surgical procedures, pharmaceuticals, medical devices, and other ways of keeping consumers well or treating them when they are diseased or injured.

Technology not only alleviates many of the problems created by the absence of good health, it has increased average life expectancy from 24 years during the Roman Empire and 46 years in the early 1900s to 78 years today. While consumer expectations for technology run the risk of outpacing its development and implementation, the greater danger is that people who could benefit from life-saving technology may not receive it because it is simply too expensive to widely deploy.

Economics

The purpose of an economic system is to maximize available resources (traditionally described as land, labor, and capital) to meet the needs and wants of a nation's citizens, as well as provide an allocation process to determine whose needs and wants are fulfilled. We cannot solve America's "Two Trillion Dollar Crisis" without examining basic economic principles, especially the role of consumers in a free-market economy in directing resource creation and allocation.

The most fundamental principle of economics is the relationship between supply and demand. Years ago, Dr. Blackwell was involved in determining how many primary care and specialty physicians were needed in the rural and urban areas of Ohio. Such might seem like a simple process of calculating the number and age distribution of people in each county. The disturbing conclusion, however, was that demand is determined more by supply than vice versa. When money is available for any level of health care desired by consumers (paid by third parties), there is almost no limit to how much consumers will "need" or "want." Since there can never be enough supply of health care personnel, facilities and pharmaceuticals to fulfill demand, consumers place unrelenting pressure to spend an increasing proportion of the nation's resources on health care, especially when they believe "everyone" is entitled to all the health care they want or need and "someone else" should pay.

Insatiability of demand is a familiar concept to economists and consumer behavior analysts. Consider the family that earns $60,000 a year and can't pay for everything it needs and wants. The family might believe that if it earned only a little more—perhaps another $10,000-all of its needs and wants would be satisfied. When income increases, however, so does the perception of what the family "needs" and even affluent families find themselves spending more than they earn. Financial experts advise such families, "Don't start with what you want in planning your budget; start with what you earn." Families who spend more than they earn often end up deprived of things they really do need—health care, of course, but also perhaps food, cars, clothing or homes—and 1.6 million of them in 2003 ended up in bankruptcy, the same place America's health care system is headed. Spending what a nation needs or wants rather than what it can afford underlies America's "Two Trillion Dollar Crisis." So, who should decide how much of the nation's resources should be spent on health care and who should receive what levels of care? That changes with the transition to consumer driven health care.

Ways to Allocate Health Care Resources

How does a nation have jobs and prosperity if it devotes too high a proportion of its resources to health care? Given that an economy never has enough resources to supply all of a nation's needs and wants, how should health care resources be allocated?

One way is by lottery. Many consumers willingly pay a dollar for a "Powerball" chance of winning $200 million. We also have lotteries in some urban public schools with such scarce resources as alternative, magnet or language-immersion programs. Rather than try to decide which students merit these programs, school districts simply hold a drawing. To some degree, that's the way it's done for some types of health care. With only a limited number of vital organs available for transplant, for example, should they be allocated to the "wealthy," the "worthy," or the "lucky?"

Another way is centralized planning. During much of the last century, the U.S.S.R., China, Cuba, and North Korea allocated resources according to the Marxist ideal of "from everyone according to his abilities, to everyone according to his needs." Although there are many appealing aspects of letting the government assume the role of funding, controlling or directing the health care systems, there are important caveats and lessons to be considered from the economics of central planning compared to market direction that occurs in consumer driven health care.

In a divided Germany, two countries sharing the same language, culture, and resources (East Germany actually had the better land and other historical advantages) operated under the alternatives of market and central planning. The citizens of East Germany could figuratively look across the Wall (literally with the advent of TV), and see their cousins in a market-driven society. What they saw eventually brought the Wall tumbling down. The reason communism failed is that such centrally planned systems are terribly inefficient at creating economic resources.

While many Americans believe we have a market-driven system for health care, in reality the cost of routine everyday health care is paid by third-party payers instead of consumers. Insurers, employers, and government (Medicare/Medicaid) define which diagnostic tests, procedures, medications and length of stays are covered, often based on Diagnostic Related Groups (DRGs). The result is what Chapter 7 describes as the "evils of first dollar consumer coverage." No wise consumer would buy zero-deductible auto insurance because the cost would be too high, yet first-dollar coverage is a major reason why health insurance is so expensive and why the health care system is so inefficient. Consumers may believe they should have whatever they need to get well, but only affluent consumers can truly act on their beliefs. What everyone else receives is determined by the rules of plans administered by third-party payers.

The bottom line is that an understanding of economics is an essential component to analyzing health care costs. The direction is beginning to reverse from third-party payers making those decisions to consumer driven health care. In a market system, consumers who earn more or who save more of what they earn have the economic ability to negotiate directly with health care providers when they want more than what a third-party payer allows.

Culture and Consumer Lifestyles

How many resources should be devoted to preserving the life of a premature baby? The prevailing culture—including ethical and religious norms—affects not only who lives, but the proportion of the nation's economic resources devoted to sustaining that life, perhaps for decades in the future. Similar decisions occur at the other end of life. If a person does not have the ability to pay their health care expenses, should a $250,000 surgical procedure be performed and paid for by others for people age 65? 75? 85? 95? At what age and expense level should extraordinary or even ordinary life support systems be terminated?

Culture refers to the *values, ideas, artifacts, and symbols that help individuals communicate, interpret, and evaluate as members of society.* It is the "blueprint" of human activity, determining the coordinates of social interaction and productive activity, influenced by ethnicity, race, religion, and national or regional identity. As a result, culture determines much of the health of individuals and the standards of health care that prevail in a nation.

If health care can be provided in a private room costing $2,500 per day, $1,500 per day in a semi-private room, or $250 a day in a ward with 50 or more people, what is the appropriate level of care for those who cannot pay from their own resources? If the nursing shortage could be partially solved by encouraging citizens from other countries to immigrate to the United States and perform those services, perhaps at one-third the cost of existing nurses, should laws be changed to encourage this practice? Or, if nursing care can be provided in the hospital by family or friends (as it is in many other nations), should the health care system be expected to pay hospital employees to provide those same services? What if services by paid employees are of a lesser quality than could be provided by a patient's family?

Culture also determines consumer lifestyles—the greatest determinant of health care costs, described in Chapter 8. Perhaps no consumer lifestyle factor affects health care costs as much as obesity, with nearly 65 percent of American consumers either obese or overweight. The link between obesity and diabetes, heart disease, cancer, and many other diseases is well-established, as are the added costs of providing health care for these consumers. Many hospitals now have to buy reinforced beds, rebuild bathrooms, or spend $4,000 per wheelchair to accommodate patients weighing 800 pounds or more (regular wheelchairs cost $400). Should obese patients have to cover these extra costs or are you willing to pay more for them?

In recent years, the most visible cultural shift in regards to lifestyle choices has been with cigarette smoking. Prohibitions in public places, warning labels, and media awareness of the health risks have all contributed to significant decline in the proportion of adults who smoke. As excise taxes cause cigarettes to reach $7 to $7.50 a pack in New York and other cities, many consumers have decided the cost just isn't worth it. The result has been a corresponding decline in cancer, heart disease and other maladies linked to tobacco use. Will Americans attack obesity with the same vigor?

Dr. William Malarkey in his fascinating book *Take Control of Your Aging* describes his experiences in retirement homes where it is not uncommon to see people who have celebrated 100 or more years of life. He observes that few, if any, are overweight. With lawsuits aimed at fast-food restaurants (mostly unsuccessful because the defense is that obesity is a decision of consumers, not food providers), TV shows and magazines describing better nutrition, and a president who exercises regularly, it might be hoped that America would be winning the war on obesity—but as you'll read in Chapter 9, the statistics don't yet indicate much progress.

Legal and Political Factors

To some degree, legal and political factors embody the other three components (technology, economics, and culture) and provide guidance on how to create and allocate health care resources. Should the process be government funded, government regulated, or government guided?

Contracts, including those between employers and employees, employers and insurers, insurers and health care providers, governments and citizens, and Medicare/Medicaid and health care providers determine how much health care costs and how costs are controlled. Reform of the health care system necessarily involves revision of many existing contracts, not a process eagerly embraced by the involved parties (particularly those making money from the current system).

Other components of the legal system affect both personal health and health care. The cost of malpractice insurance is one of the most troubling. If frivolous lawsuits cause a physician's malpractice insurance premiums to double or triple, some might conclude that the increase is paid by physicians, but in the end, it is paid by consumers. As physicians flee regions with out-of-control malpractice insurance costs, some consumers might find it necessary to travel hundreds of miles to get the care they need. Others pay exorbitant prices for unnecessary diagnostic tests ordered by physicians looking to "protect" themselves from the risk of malpractice lawsuits (also known as practicing "defensive medicine").

Despite the proven effectiveness of preventive medicine in extending longevity and improving quality of life, prevention requires an up-front investment that often diverts funds available for those in the business of curative medicine. And unlike medical treatment that brings an immediate result, the benefits of prevention may not be realized for years. For example, implementing a program that offers free medicine and supplies to diabetics who participate in monthly counseling sessions at a pharmacy requires a large up-front budget. But if the program can reduce the life-long treatment of high blood pressure, blindness, and kidney failure that can result from uncontrolled diabetes, while also increasing productivity by enabling people to return to work, doesn't it actually save money in the long-term? As illustrated in Exhibit 1.4, a 10 percent decrease in the leading causes of death would reduce health care costs by $17 billion over the span of the lives saved. Sadly, when many states are nearly bankrupt from Medicaid obligations, they argue they cannot afford the cost of such health-promoting programs.

Solutions to America's "Two Trillion Dollar Crisis"

The purpose of this book is to generate a dialog among concerned citizens, health care providers and policymakers about the U.S.

Exhibit 1.4   Less Pain, More Gain; Reining in these common killers in the United States would be worth trillions of dollars

$17 TRILLION University of Chicago researchers Kevin Murphy and Robert H. Topel have shown that a permanent 16 percent decrease in major U.S. causes of death could add trillions of dollars of economic value in the United States the span of the lives saved.

Cause of Death	Potential U.S. Gain (millions of dollars)
Major cardiovascular diseases	$ 5,142
Malignant neoplasms	4,359
Infectious diseases (including AIDS)	644
Chronic obstructive pulmonary diseases	605
Pneumonia and influenza	388
Diabetes	449
Chronic liver disease and cirrhosis	310
Accidents and adverse effects	1,389
Homocide and legal intervention	413
Suicide	508
Other	3,006
Total	$17,163

health care system and how health care can be reformed by consumers. The objective is to understand the depth of the crisis, how it has developed, and why the shift to consumer driven health care is inevitable.

The next chapter shows how the economy can perform well on nearly every objective measure, yet headlines report continued joblessness. Rather than hire additional employees incurring health care costs, firms are finding other ways to remain competitive. Chapter 2 documents how high health care costs affect the ability of Americans to have jobs, build profitable companies and maintain the high levels of consumption they have achieved over the past century.

Chapter 3 reveals why American consumers should scour the globe for innovative solutions. There is much to be learned from the policies, technology, and lifestyles that allow consumers elsewhere to live longer and pay less. One model can be seen in Singapore, which expends only 3.9 percent of its GDP on health care but attains universal coverage and high individual longevity. Chapter 3 shows how to implement the world's best practices while avoiding the worst.

Chapters 4 and 5 provide the "nitty-gritty" ways the American health care system can be reformed and improved when consumers are in control. Although there are plenty of examples of progress already occurring, such pacesetting solutions need to be implemented throughout the nation. To do that, there must be widespread understanding of not only *how* they work, but *why* they work.

The natural tendency of people is to resist change, but once effective solutions are properly understood what is likely to happen can be predicted. Chapter 6 explains that just as power in retail has shifted from general department stores (attempting to be everything to everyone) to the coexistence of niche specialty stores and superefficient mass retailers, power will shift from general practitioners and hospitals to new and innovative channels of health care delivery.

In Chapter 7, you'll learn why a Health Savings Account eliminates the pitfalls of bad insurance—first-dollar coverage for routine expenditures—and in Chapters 8 and 9, you'll learn why consumers are the only ones who can conquer the costs of health care with "miracle cures" focused on preventive rather than curative medicine.

Many of the answers proposed in the following pages create disruption and dislocation of present personnel and facilities, a process that is certain to arouse emotion and generate resistance. Read the warning label at the beginning of Chapter 6, for instance, if you are a hospital administrator or employee. But strategies are not wrong just because they are disruptive and dislocative. The management and staff of Montgomery Ward and K-Mart were not enthusiastic supporters of the rising market share of mass retailers like Wal-Mart and Target but consumers voted with their wallets and the most consumer-centric and efficient retail models prevailed. That same process will happen, and already is happening, in health care when consumers "vote" with their wallets. The result will be a health care system that is not only more efficient, but one that delivers an improved level of quality and satisfaction to consumers.

The outcome of shifting from a third-party payer system to consumer driven health care is shown in the diagram on the back cover. Major processes include the following themes that, interwoven together, accomplish the overall goal of better health and lower costs.

1. Existing health care institutions will be forced to become more efficient or they won't survive when consumers pay most of their routine health care bills in a consumer driven

health care system. The incentive for consumers to demand change is provided by a Health Savings Account, designed to eliminate the evils of "first dollar" or low-deductible health insurance policies.

2. "Global thinking" is just as important to health care delivery as it is in business, economics, and national policy.

3. Consumer driven health care will cause the same polarity in the distribution of health care services and products in the twenty-first century that consumers caused in the distribution of other goods and services during the twentieth century.

4. Major decreases in health care costs and major improvements in health occur when consumers and employers are both rewarded for better health, and a Health Savings Account is a catalyst for that to happen.

5. The improvements in the health care system caused by consumer driven health care will make it possible to provide the uninsured with affordable health insurance, will help employers create more jobs instead of more layoffs, and will reduce the proportion of GDP devoted to health care sufficiently to allow more spending on other societal and consumer needs.

By the time you finish reading this book, you may conclude that America's "Two Trillion Dollar Crisis" is solvable, if approached analytically. The solutions outlined in this book could reduce the proportion of GDP devoted to health care by several percentage points, and perhaps even to levels competitive with other industrialized countries. These changes will not come easily or on their own. The catalyst will be consumers with the power to buy. As consumers assume control of their health care expenditures, eventually they will force health care institutions to provide the products and services they want, at prices they are willing to pay, creating an open consumer marketplace for health care.

CHAPTER 2

Is Your Job Next to Go?

"For every complex problem there is a simple solution that is wrong."
—George Bernard Shaw

Few topics are as important to us as our jobs—what we do, what we're paid, and most critical, will we still be needed in the future? How can the economy do so well—producing more goods and services and higher incomes for most people—while headlines report layoffs and persistent unemployment? What's happening? And more important, what does it mean to you? As you look for answers to these questions, you'll find the cost of health care lurking in the background. This chapter shows how an economy can grow without creating any new jobs, how rising health care costs threaten future jobs, why small business will be one of the strongest advocates of consumer driven health care, and why a Health Savings Account is a valuable tool in job creation and winning the war on health care costs.

Be Productive or Be Gone

In an era of intense global competition, there are three ways for firms to generate higher profits. First is to increase demand by creating new products and services that consumers find valuable, or by convincing consumers to increase consumption and pay more for existing products and services. Both are accomplished by superior marketing including branding and supply chain management.

The second way to increase profits is to lower input costs such as raw materials, capital, and labor. However, when commodities and other materials are sourced globally at near uniform prices and capital flows across national borders in nanoseconds, these inputs become "constants," leaving labor cost as the major differentiator among nations. In globalization, jobs migrate to nations with the lowest wages and benefits costs, accounting for 300,000 of the 2.7 million U.S. jobs lost between 2000 and 2004 according to Forrester Research. While transportation costs (which include the cost of financing in-transit goods and the risk of unreliable delivery) sometimes overcome labor cost advantages to moving jobs offshore, this is not an issue if the "product" is a service that can be "transported" by telephone, Internet, or satellite.

The third way to raise profits is to increase productivity by creating more products and services with existing labor and other resources. Because "labor input costs" include "benefits"—mostly employer-sponsored health insurance—firms face agonizing questions as to whether new people are necessary. Should a firm hire a new worker incurring an average of $7,000 to $10,000 in health care costs or should it increase overtime for existing employees adding no new benefits? Should it add a new worker in the United States or outsource to other nations where employees sometimes have better health care and always have lower health care costs? Or, is it possible for a firm to re-engineer its operations and supply chain functions to obtain greater output with fewer employees? If health care costs are not reduced, there is little question where jobs will go in the future, as illustrated by the following scenario.

Globalization 101

The time is 1950. The scene is Portsmouth, Ohio, population 43,000. The seat of Scioto County on the Ohio River, Portsmouth is a typical middle-American manufacturing community with three large employers: the Wheeling Steel Company, the Selby Shoe Company, and the Williams Manufacturing Company.

Wheeling Steel has 3,500 unionized employees, paid an average of $3.50 an hour, who produce commercial building materials for the construction market. The Selby Shoe Company, founded in 1884, also has 3,500 unionized employees, producing moderately priced women's shoes. The Williams Manufacturing Company employs 2,300 nonunion employees at an average rate of $1.65 an hour, producing approximately 10,000,000 pairs of lower priced shoes per year.

Fast forward 50 years to today. Portsmouth's population is reduced over 50 percent to 21,000. The Wheeling Steel plant was torn down years ago when competition from higher quality and lower-priced imported steel caused its 3,500 jobs to vanish. The Selby Shoe

Company was liquidated after a labor strike in 1953. Its former brands, Selby and Naturalizer, still are sold in the US, but are sourced by the Brown Shoe Company from a network of global suppliers. As the marketing of low priced women's shoes moved from small, locally-owned shoe stores to large chains with enormous buying power, Williams Manufacturing could no longer produce at a labor price point low enough to compete in the U.S. market and likewise closed its doors.

Portsmouth's decline illustrates the fundamental principle of globalization: if workers are competent in other places and the legal and logistics infrastructure is in place, work will migrate to the lowest cost producers. Congress can pass laws, and unions can organize strikes to delay job movement, but neither can deny the laws of economics. If a domestic producer cannot increase its productivity, reduce its costs (including health care costs), develop better products than global competitors, or market its products to consumers who are willing to pay premium prices reflecting higher costs, that firm first loses profits, then loses jobs, and finally goes out of business.

A common solution to the "outsourcing problem" is to ask consumers to "Buy American." Some observers ask, "Wouldn't consumers be willing to pay higher prices to support American workers?" From PCs to pantyhose, consumers who vote with their wallets on a daily basis have responded: "No!" A few years ago, Wal-Mart tried to maintain a policy of "Buy American," perhaps believing consumers would pay a little more for American-made products. However, when it started losing business to competitors selling cheaper goods made in China, Wal-Mart placed lower priced imports next to its higher priced American-made products and found consumers almost always purchased the cheaper goods. Consumers may *say* they prefer to "Buy American," but their true attitudes are reflected in their actions every time the cash registers ring up another import at Wal-Mart. Understanding what is happening to jobs in the U.S. economy is critically important to understanding why we need to reduce health care costs.

Health Care Costs Can Be Life-Threatening to Organizations

Look closely at financial statements of most firms and you'll find *decreasing* costs of overhead, manufacturing, logistics and other costs, but the one line that is *increasing*—usually at double-digit rates—is health care. Annual health care expenditures per worker increased from $4,430 to $6,615 in 2003, as shown in Exhibit 2.1, and have nearly doubled in the past decade. Some studies indicate that the cost of health insurance for a single worker today averages $7,000 ($10,000 for family coverage). Extrapolate that a few years forward and, unless there's widespread acceptance of solutions described in this book, health care costs could easily be half the salaries of many U.S. workers.

Exhibit 2.1   Costs Continue to Rise

Note: Includes all medical, dental, and other health benefits, for all covered employees and dependents. Includes employer and employee contributions.

Source: Mercer Natio

Firms cope by hiring fewer people. In the past, increasing production in response to greater demand meant adding workers. Today, output is increased using technology—with costs known, fixed, and recoverable in six to 18 months. If gross domestic product increases three to five percent a year, a respectable level in the view of most economists, factories and service organizations will increase their output. But with manufacturing capacity around 70 percent, most can increase production without adding many, or perhaps any, new employees. In fact, a 1.3 percent increase in productivity results in one million fewer jobs in the types of large firms included in government employment data.

For example, a bakery employing 600 employees invests in a robot that moves products from the production line into boxes for shipping, replacing 40 workers on three shifts. These are unskilled, low-paid workers, earning about $20,000 a year, but their health care costs average over $6,000 a year—the same as management. The robot incurs no health care expense (except a little oil and some occasional software upgrades), doesn't call in sick, and will work three shifts a day without asking for overtime pay. It may seem heartless to replace 40 workers with a robot, but doing so keeps costs low enough to sell the firm's products in the United States and other countries, protecting the jobs of the remaining employees.

Remember, when the unemployment rate is five percent, the employment rate is 95 percent. Although both candidates in the 2004 presidential election promised to end the nation's "5.4 percent unemployment problem," a "structural" unemployment rate of four to five percent is considered by most economists to be normal and that from 1948 to 2000, U.S. unemployment averaged 5.6 percent. Reducing unemployment much below those levels is likely to cause inflation, declining productivity, and even recession. That's what happened in the last quarter of 2000, creating the need for tax cuts and other economic policies to recover. European nations like Germany contending with double-digit unemployment are still envious of U.S. unemployment rates that are among the lowest in the world.

Actually, large numbers of the self-employed and employees of small companies are overlooked in government employment data based on the payrolls of the 400,000 largest employers tracked by the Department of Labor. Headlines are made when one large firm like AT&T eliminates 12,000 positions, yet it goes unreported when 12,000 small firms each add one new worker. From January 2001 through mid-2004, government employment data report the nation lost 900,000 jobs, but household data (which includes employees of small businesses, farms and newly formed entrepreneurial businesses) report a net increase of 1.9 million jobs. Few people know that 430,000 people currently make their living on eBay, more than the total number of employees of General Electric and Procter & Gamble combined. Labor Department statistics don't count these workers in its jobs data, but the fact of the matter is that self-employment and small business creates most of the jobs that reduce unemployment.

Thanks to increases in productivity, more people are making more money than ever, gross domestic product (GDP) and disposable personal income (DPI) gains are better than at any time in the last 20 years and there have been similar increases in capital investment, manufacturing activity, retail sales, homeownership, and consumer confidence. Inflation and interest rates are still at historic lows and even the stock market has performed well, not just from increasing corporate profits, but by consumer willingness to invest, especially when they are concerned about the future of their jobs, their pensions, Social Security and Medicare. Even the deficit is alleviated by rising tax revenues based on higher incomes and corporate profits. Further help comes from a weak U.S. dollar, encouraging exports and curtailing imports of higher priced foreign goods, benefiting U.S. producers and perhaps creating a few more jobs.

Is the cost of employee health insurance really out of control, or is it simply increasing similar to other economic measures? The relative costs of health care are shown in Exhibit 2.2. Workers' earnings, overall inflation and even the Medical Consumer Price Index (MCPI) have increased at relatively stable rates but health insurance premiums have soared to a rate currently four times the MCPI and seven times overall inflation. If the MCPI, which includes the retail prices of commodities such as prescription and over-the-counter drugs, medical supplies, equipment, and service providers including physicians, dentists, and nursing homes, remains constant, then Americans must be consuming more health care—creating a tremendous burden on employers.

Despite being the greatest creators of new jobs, small businesses face health insurance costs increasing two to three percent faster than large firms, primarily because large firms have greater power to secure "volume" discounts from health care providers. While monthly insurance premiums for the nation's employers rose 13.9 percent in 2003, the increase was 15.6 percent among small firms, with some experiencing spikes as high as 40 to 60 percent a year according to the Kaiser Family Foundation. In recent years, rising health care costs have dampened payroll gains, as illustrated in Exhibit 2.3. Nonfarm jobs increased regularly until health care costs spiked in 1999, and then employment soon leveled off. No one should really be surprised that a recovering economy has failed to produce many new jobs when health care costs are rising at double digit rates.

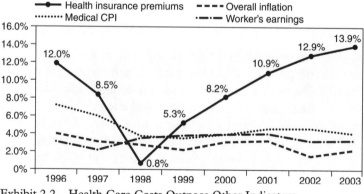

Exhibit 2.2   Health Care Costs Outpace Other Indicators

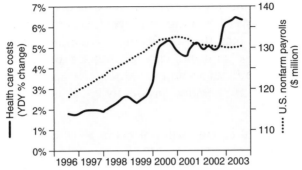

Exhibit 2.3   Unhealthy Job Gains? Surging health care costs in recent years have helped damp payroll gains. Source: Labor Department.

Fortunately, some firms fight back! One example can be found in Elgin, Illinois, where the Middleby Corporation is performing a modern workplace miracle. This maker of ovens and toasters for the restaurant industry is a rare breed of U.S. manufacturer. Of its five factories, four are in the United States. Despite low-cost overseas competition and rocketing employee benefits costs at home, revenue has grown 14 percent and earnings per share have zoomed at a 121 percent annual rate the past five years (*Investors Business Daily,* March 18, 2004). Middleby's strategy is to increase efficiency by creating a uniform platform for its line of stackable ovens sold under the flagship Middleby Marshall brand, giving it faster output and bigger economies of scale.

As sales continue to grow, however, Middleby has all but avoided expanding its payroll. How? Middleby relies on overtime, which accrues no new added health care benefits expense, to squeeze greater productivity out of its existing work force. Many of Middleby's 1,000 workers are also cross-trained in different jobs, allowing them to work for peers absent to vacation or illness.

Management, employees and unions clinging to the practices of the past probably face a future of failure. Firms like Middleby and thousands others that plan to succeed follow a few basic principles:

1. Involvement of all employees at every level in understanding the nature of global competition and that to survive the firm must be efficient and reduce costs
2. Company-wide focus on serving customers better than competitors

3. Sharing of health care insurance costs between employer and employees, helping employers reduce costs and helping employees reap the benefits of maintaining better health
4. A "cafeteria" of health care insurance programs to fit the needs of individuals and rewarding the ones achieving better health and personal productivity

In the end, real change will not occur until health care evolves from "someone else" paying the bills to consumer driven health care in which routine health care expenses are paid, and therefore scrutinized, by consumers.

Employers still pay the bulk of health insurance premiums—typically 75 percent—but are gradually shifting more costs to workers, in hopes of lowering expense by discouraging unnecessary use of doctors, hospitals and prescription drugs. Deductibles and co-payments, which were uncommon only a few years ago, are now required by 40 percent of benefit plans, causing employees' share of health care costs to rise by 48 percent between 2000 and 2003. As an even greater percentage is shifted to consumers, they too will feel the pain of rising health care costs and enlist in the fight to lower health care costs, but many will also realize the benefits when they have a high deductible insurance policy with their savings banked in a Health Savings Account.

Solution to America's "Two Trillion Dollar Crisis": Shift costs of ordinary, routine health care from employers and their insurance companies to health care users.

Workers in small firms feel the greatest pain from rising health care costs but they also benefit most from consumer driven health care. In the "old" economy, large firms made employees dependent on health insurance coverage provided as an employee benefit. The "new" economy creates jobs in small businesses where employees must shop for their own health insurance and pay for it with their own money—making it "portable" from one employer to another.

Today, many self-employed and small business workers are running bare, coping with the high costs of health care by not buying health insurance or, for the fortunate ones, seeking coverage from their spouse's employer. Some are among America's 45 million people with no health insurance. These uninsured are the heart of America's economy and they need help! For them, a high-deductible policy coupled with a Health Savings Account provides a good solution at a price they can afford. (How HSAs work is explained in Chapter 7.)

Finding Your Next Job

When corporate restructuring threatens jobs, many people have little choice except to restructure themselves. Individuals have to change their skills, motivation and expectations, develop different work patterns, and perhaps accept a different type of job, lower wages, or even start their own business. The message is not popular but it's a lot more realistic than telling people to wait until things improve to be reinstated in their previous "old economy" jobs.

Some sectors of the economy are desperately seeking workers. As you will read in Chapter 5, one of the most visible is nursing with 1.1 million new jobs projected between 2002 and 2012, according to the U.S. Department of Labor. Increased demand for skilled nurses due to an aging population means that if no additional nurses are trained, wages will soar and quality of care will plummet. Nursing does not necessarily require a college degree, but it does require specialized training and a willingness to do sometimes unpleasant work helping others. It also makes a direct contribution to solving America's "Two Trillion Dollar Crisis."

Nursing a Nation's Economy Back to Health

Spending relatively small amounts of money to increase the supply of qualified nurses pays big dividends by reducing direct health care costs for several decades. Increasing the capacity of nurse training programs also helps solve the problem of a jobless economy, because the one-on-one, hands-on care provided by nurses cannot easily be shipped overseas or conducted over the Internet.

In Maryland, the supply of registered nurses is projected to fall short of demand by 27 percent (or 13,000 nurses) by 2015, according to the U.S. Department of Health and Human Services. To meet this demand,

Howard Community College in Columbia has started a 12–month fast-track option, allowing qualified RN students to graduate in half the traditional two years by taking classes during summer and winter breaks. Other schools are adding spring admissions and 18–month accelerated programs. Some applicants are fresh from high school, some have bachelor's degrees in unrelated fields where employment is sparse, and some are in their 40s and 50s, finally able to return to the workforce helping others for the 20 to 30 years of their remaining economic lives.

Job retraining programs work. The PBS documentary "Company Town" shows what happened in Canton, Ohio after Maytag Corporation closed its Hoover manufacturing plant. One of the former employees, Jeff Ring, suddenly realized he was a high school-educated, unemployed factory worker with a ponytail, beard, and usually wearing a T-shirt. People encouraged him to become a welder or auto body shop technician because of his background and appearance. Instead, he restructured himself, enrolling in nursing school to become a critical care nurse. In the documentary, Ring explained, "I can see why you don't want this guy (himself) as a nurse. No, this is not acceptable for male nursing students. I just cut my ponytail off and trimmed up to the corporate goatee and that's it. Now I'm this version. I'm sure that just about everybody that heard about it assumed that I'd be flunked out of the program in the first six months. I'm sure that they didn't think I was going to stick with it. When you work at the steel foundry, you don't even talk to anybody else for hours at a time. You're just in your own head. I should have been doing something in the medical field a long time ago. Actually, I'm participating in society for a change."

Jeff Ring "gets it." Millions of other Americans must also "get it" if the nation is going to reduce unemployment and address the shortage of skilled labor in health care. Believing jobs will automatically be created by an improved economy is as dangerous as a physician prescribing treatment without making a diagnosis. Restructuring worker abilities is not an easy solution to sell, but it's the most realistic solution to both job creation and health care costs.

> *Solution to America's "Two Trillion Dollar Crisis": Additional funding from federal, state and private organizations to increase the number of qualified nurses, mostly funding post-secondary educational institutions appealing to nontraditional college students.*

The Demographics of Demand for Health Care

In the analysis of consumer spending, demographics determine about two-thirds of everything, from the products people buy, to where they buy them and how they use them. Health care is no exception. The demand for specific health care services can be found at any age although demand generally rises as people get older. As with other products, the age group that provides the greatest understanding of immediate future of health care costs is the "baby boomers."

The Baby Boomer Effect

After World War II, beginning in 1946, the nation went on a re-creation spree, resulting in over four million births per year until 1965, when the number dropped to 3.7 million. The smaller number of consumers born later, about 41 million between 1968 and 1979, were to some degree forgotten (labeled "Generation X") and those born in the '80s and '90s followed suit and were called "Generation Y."

The "baby boom" moves through markets like an invading army, requiring marketers to satisfy the needs, wants, and fantasies of 76 million people. Boomers not only affect the economy; they *are* the economy, representing the greatest share of the work force, the greatest share of income, and the greatest share of voting power and political influence. Baby boomers were prosperous during the 1980s and '90s but they spent more than they earned, buying products that past generations considered luxuries, such as consumer electronics, vacation homes and household services. They drove the mini-van market in the 1980s, the SUV market in the 1990s, and are driving the resurrection of the sporty convertible in the 2000s. According to U.S. Census projections, the number of people age 45 to 54 is projected to increase 14 percent between 2001 and 2010, while the number of 55–64 year olds, the age when individual health care costs start to soar, will grow by a whopping 44 percent. During the same decade, consumers in the 25 to 34 and 35 to 44 age brackets (the most productive years of life) are projected to *decline*. Since Social Security and Medicare tax the income of younger generations to support social spending for older generations, the United States is facing a potential problem.

There's still time to make changes, but after around 2010, massive numbers of consumers will move to an age when traditionally they expect to retire, mostly with income from Social Security. At that time, millions of boomers will start visiting doctors and hospitals as often as they visit golf courses and cruise ships. Unless things change, it's possible that federal spending on Social Security and Medicare could eventually consume as much of the nation's economy as the entire federal budget does now, gobbling up the entire incomes of younger consumers.

The Most Powerful Person in Washington

If you asked the question, "Who's the most powerful person in Washington?" casual observers might reply "the President." More astute observers would probably answer, "Alan Greenspan." The words of this Federal Reserve Board Chairman move markets and push politicians to defend their policies. At the height of the stock market bubble in 2000, Greenspan calmly noted that the market was exhibiting "irrational exuberance." If more investors had listened and purchased stocks with "profits" instead of "prophets," they might not have seen their portfolios cut in half. Greenspan's words about how your future health care is financed will also influence America's ability to compete in a global economy, a key to protecting jobs.

Greenspan provoked a political tempest when he told members of the House Budget Committee that future Social Security and Medicare benefits must be reduced to prevent a fiscal calamity in decades to come. While the ability to meet Social Security obligations has concerned people for years, Greenspan warned that Medicare entitlements, which are "unknown" and "unlimited," are a much more serious concern than Social Security benefits which are "defined" and "actuarially predictable." In addition, medical science not only leads to more expensive treatments, but allows people with chronic conditions to live longer, incurring greater health care costs.

Experts forecast future deficits for Social Security and Medicare to be in the trillions, increasing each year nothing is done. The problems would be acute even if today's federal budget were balanced, but budget deficits make matters worse because the government is borrowing more than $200 billion a year from the Social Security and Medicare trust funds (surpluses that are supposed to be accumulating to pay benefits when baby boomers retire) to finance its current operating expenses. We are potentially creating the most colossal financial train wreck the nation has ever experienced.

When it comes to being able to pay for your health care in the future, don't count on your employer or the government. If you are reading this book and under the age of 50, the safest course of action is to start planning now for a future where the government may not be a reliable source of retirement income beyond some minimal subsistence level. Not only must younger generations demand changes in these government programs, they must also aggressively fund their Health Savings Accounts while their health costs are low to be sure they are taken care of when they are old. In consumer driven health care, your future health care (and your future standard of living) will be determined mostly by what you do today.

What's the Solution?

As the quotation attributed to George Bernard Shaw at the beginning of this chapter indicates, "for every complex problem there is a simple solution that is wrong." Relying on simple solutions won't solve the problems caused by the escalating numbers of people heading toward both retirement and high health care costs. Baby boomers spent their money on the "good life" and failed to save much for either retirement income or increased medical costs. The rest of the nation will either have to pay for their failure, deny them the benefits to which they thought they were entitled, or change the system.

It seems unlikely the voters of America or their political leaders will deny health care and retirement benefits to people already receiving or nearing the age when they expect to receive benefits. But the jobs of all young people are at stake if health care costs continue to rise above their current 15 percent level. It's better to change the system, and that's what consumer driven health care is all about.

Origin of the Pension

Otto von Bismarck, the "Iron Chancellor" of Germany, decided in the late 1800s that army officers who survived to age 65 shouldn't have to remain in the battlefield but should be allowed to live the rest of their lives with a secure income, which he called a *pension*. Such was the precedent in the 1930s when the United States enacted Social Security (and later Medicare) with 65 as the "retirement age." The pension was primarily for farmers and factory workers who survived well beyond the normal life expectancy (about 50 at the time) because they were physically no longer able to do the manual labor required to hold a job. If we used the same logic today, the appropriate age for the government to begin supporting retirees would be 76!

At one time, the "gold watch" also meant a life in a rocking chair. No longer is that the norm. With better health than past generations, and a secure income from Social Security, most retirees can look forward to decades of fun and leisure, more likely being "rock stars" than "rockers." They could, however, probably work a few years more, taking early retirement only if they had planned their savings program—for both income and medical care—appropriately over their former decades of work.

The most significant solution to reducing Medicare and Social Security deficits is to adjust further the age at which Social Security and Medicare benefits begin. If you think 65 is the normal retirement age for Social Security, and you were born before 1938, you are correct. However, if you were born later than that date, you might not be aware that the present schedule was changed a few years ago to make 67 the official age for full Social Security benefits, with a sliding scale for retirement benefits depending on date of birth. That requires changing the age people and organizations expect to retire, a major shift in cultural norms and work patterns.

Since mortality rates accelerate after age 65, increasing the retirement age reduces substantially the number of people who will ever receive benefits as well as the number of years the system pays recipients. Because the largest health care expenditures occur later in life, however, this does not necessarily benefit an employer if it means incurring an employee's most expensive, terminal illnesses. That's why it's important for individuals also to have their own savings for health care expenses banked in a Health Savings Account.

Quasi-Retirement

In America, careers usually progress on the "up or out" principle, and when supervisors or senior managers approach "normal" retirement, it usually means "out." But in many other countries, it's culturally acceptable for senior managers to resign their positions and return to lower levels, such as engineer or accountant, held prior to promotion.

Quasi-retirement helps employees, employers and society by advancing the age of full retirement. A few firms are already using highly experienced workers who might otherwise retire to fill in for younger workers during vacations, sabbaticals, training, or maternity leaves. Other firms are "doubling up" by employing two quasi-retired workers for one job, recognizing their desire for increased leisure time and receiving in return, the wisdom, reliability and dedication of long-term employees. Less concerned about future promotions, quasi-retired workers are especially useful for special projects that younger workers might not be capable of handling or are reluctant to accept with no clear career path.

Firms can reduce total health care costs by adopting innovative approaches to encourage quasi-retirement beyond age 65. The health insurance cost per employee for workers on Medicare is typically hundreds of dollars less per month than the cost for young or middle-aged workers, making firms more profitable. The Medicare system also benefits from lower costs because working people over 65 are typically healthier than if they were not working. Studies indicate that continuing employment past age 65 keeps people socially engaged, mentally active and generally in better physical shape. Younger workers pay less of their salaries for Medicare and Social Security, and the national brain and skill drain likely to be caused by large numbers of retiring baby boomers is somewhat alleviated. But will people be happier working in quasi-retirement jobs than if they were fully retired? That depends, of course, on personal expectations, social norms, corporate policies, union and government regulations, and the national understanding of America's "Two Trillion Dollar Crisis."

> *Solution to America's "Two Trillion Dollar Crisis": Increase the age at which Medicare and Social Security benefits are received and change organizational retirement policies and programs to encourage quasi-retirement.*

If Americans choose to retain Medicare as we now know it, it is nearly inevitable that the whole health care system will implode, resulting in rationing at best and bankruptcy at worst. The nurses, physicians and others who provide the labor supply to deliver health care will be so threatened by overwork that patients will suffer and U.S. companies will become noncompetitive in a global economy. Which is better? Making systematic and planned changes in the remaining years of this decade, or placing the nation in danger of bankruptcy?

It's About Passion

If you have concluded from reading this chapter that it was written by impassioned authors, you are correct. After decades of combined experience providing health care and studying health care delivery, they realize that rising health care costs are jeopardizing the economy and individual well-being. Consumer driven health care is necessary to protect jobs and assure quality health care will be available in the future. A dialogue must begin among employees, employers, health care providers, politicians, government regulators, insurers, and voters about ways to alleviate America's "Two Trillion Dollar Crisis." It's not just an academic debate. It's about jobs and health—possibly *your* job and *your* health.

CHAPTER 3

Global Thinking About Health Care

"No man is an island."
—John Donne

W hen asked if he copied ideas from other people, Wal-Mart founder Sam Walton reportedly answered, "Relentlessly, but I always try to improve upon them." Too often, Americans categorize people and organizations into "good" or "bad" and then ignore anything that challenges their perceptions. Democrats dismiss the good features of Republican policies and candidates; Republicans do the same with Democrats, and both tend to overlook their own flaws. Sam Walton didn't do that; he studied the good, bad and ugly, learning from each. As a result, he transformed the firm he founded from a single store in Rogers, Arkansas into the world's largest corporation—famous not only for low prices, but also for the speed with which it adopts innovation.

A story told by former Wal-Mart vice-chairman Donald Soderquist illustrates the process and values needed if Americans sincerely want to solve their "Two Trillion Dollar Crisis." Walton was known not only for frequent inspections of his own stores, but for a persistent presence in the stores of his competitors. In fact, Soderquist tells of a time when he and Walton walked out of a particularly inept competitor and Walton asked, "What did you learn in that store?" Soderquist replied that he observed one of the worst stores he had ever seen, to which Walton agreed, but added, "What did you see that was good?" Soderquist then proceeded to point out two features, a pantyhose display rack and an assortment of ethnic cosmetics, perhaps the only two things the competitor had done better than Wal-Mart at the time. Walton then noted the names of the suppliers so that Wal-Mart could incorporate these positive features of its competitor, and consumers rewarded the changes by choosing Wal-Mart over its competitors. That's also how health care providers will be changed as America moves toward consumer driven health care.

Borrowing the best features of others instead of bemoaning the current "bad" is the key to improving the American health care system. It's the "invisible hand" of open consumer markets that forces firms to understand and adopt best practices where ever they may be found, rewarding improvements and eliminating inefficiencies. When discussing why Canada, Germany, Japan, and other nations have health care costs dramatically lower than the United States yet often achieve more desirable results, the response of many observers is dismissive: the foreign systems are inherently different, in reality they don't work or are fraught with problems, or due to cultural differences they won't work here—all ignoring the positive elements that give those nations their competitive edge.

The United States suffers from "NIH Syndrome" in which solutions are ignored if "Not Invented Here." Although some physicians read *Lancet* and other global publications, many do not, therefore practicing without benefit of some of the world's most important, innovative research. Is there anything an American physician could learn from Asian medical journals about the effectiveness of alternative medical treatments such as acupuncture and ancient herbs, some with historic databases exceeding any in the United States? Language and cultural differences aside, many American physicians are unaware of much of the medical knowledge developed overseas. Even grants from the other NIH (National Institute of Health) are focused on pioneering domestic research instead of applying treatments and processes already proven elsewhere.

In the management of corporations and the administration of public policy, ignoring the rest of the world is a sure plan for failure. In health care, it is rare to find anyone asking, "How are these problems solved elsewhere?" but once consumers start directing how their health care dollars are spent, health care providers will look for answers wherever they can be found.

Why Be a Global Thinker?

The rapid global spread of SARS reminded everyone that today, no man or woman is an island. In nearly every nation, people are connected by the Internet, global trade, global currencies and CNN.

The world is also interconnected by international illness and medical treatment.

China is home to more than a billion people. With 30 cities expected to have more than 30 million people by 2025, China is also increasingly urbanized. People and products traveling between urban, globally connected environments allow a disease such as SARS to spread to cities around the world within hours. Global health thinkers must concern themselves with not only what can be *learned* from other countries, but also what can be *shared,* improving global health and the chances for global survival.

For managers of organizations, both large and small, three elements characterize global thinking. In *From the Edge of the World* (OSU Press, 1995), the attributes of global thinking are described as:

1. The ability to sell in global markets
2. The ability to source goods and services on a global basis
3. The ability to adopt "best practices" in management and marketing in whichever nation they may be found

The ability to sell to global markets is a skill at which U.S. firms excel. Throughout much of the world, Johnson & Johnson products can be found in nearly every home, especially homes with babies. Through mergers and marketing alliances, U.S. firms have taken market share in pharmaceuticals and precision medical devices from countries such as Switzerland and Germany. Likewise, brands such as Pepsi, McDonald's, and Sherwin-Williams cover the earth.

Global sourcing is also an attribute U.S. firms are rapidly refining, manufacturing items ranging from clothes and computers to toys and tractors wherever labor and natural resources are cheapest, or production methods are most efficient. And now it's happening in health care with major U.S. hospitals recruiting physicians and nurses trained in South Africa, the Philippines, and India where skills and knowledge can be transferred to the United States.

When health care organizations begin to analyze global best practices, they soon discover that no nation, and certainly not the United States, is best in every aspect of management and marketing. They also discover that global best practices in the management of health care reside in nearly every nation.

In manufacturing, Japan dominates production methods with firms such as Toyota, turning out cars at the highest rates of productivity and quality control in the world. Ironically, Japan adopted many of its best practices from Edward Deming, an American largely ignored in the United States until the Japanese "discovered" him. For precision watches and pharmaceuticals, Switzerland dominated for decades, providing the highest GDP per capita of the world's major economies. While nations conquered other nations with warships, the Dutch conquered commerce with trading ships. Firms such as the Dutch East Indies Company bought Manhattan Island for $34 worth of shells it collected in Indonesia, where Dutch traders had learned that stinky "black" shells covered in tar were a more valuable currency than plain white shells. Dutch best practices in commerce eventually led to the creation of one of the world's largest energy companies—Shell Oil. Today, Dutch best practices in corporate taxation allow this tiny country with few natural resources to be headquarters for multinational corporations including Philips electronics, Unilever consumer products and the world's most successful rock and roll band, the Rolling Stones.

Heart transplants didn't originate in Houston, Cleveland or Boston; they originated in South Africa, as also did many innovative plastic surgery procedures, attracting people worldwide to Cape Town for medical care. LASIK surgery, helping many Americans see and look better, originated in Greece during the late 1980s but was not approved by the FDA in the United States until 1999.

Just as Wal-Mart became stronger by incorporating the best practices of its competition, understanding and adopting the best practices of other nations is a key to strengthening the United States—whether those best practices are in operations, marketing, or health care.

The U.S. Health Care System: How Are Its Vital Statistics?

After you've entered a physician's examination room, someone usually checks your vital statistics—blood pressure, temperature, and pulse. Often blood samples are taken and analyzed, comparing your cholesterol, triglycerides or PSA to normal ranges. When the "vital statistics" of the U.S. health care system are likewise examined, fascinating results emerge.

The most comprehensive measure of a nation's health is longevity. Some might observe that longevity is not the same variable as the health care system and they would be right. In fact, most of the factors that increase longevity have little to do with the practice of medicine but rather the presence of clean air and water, adequate nutrition, education, and peace rather than war. While medical science may sustain life once illness has set in, longevity is truly a measure of "ongoing health"—all the things people do to achieve and maintain wellness as well as the system to correct for illness and accidents.

The United States is not the healthiest nation in the world, with longevity for males at 74.6 years and females at 79.8 years. The honor belongs to Japan, a nation whose citizens are concerned—some might say obsessed—with maintaining good health. Concern with health pays off, as Exhibit 3.1 reveals, with greater longevity for a number of nations, including Canada. Exhibit 3.1 shows the vital statistics for several other leading "competitors" to the United States.

How Productive Is the U.S. Health Care System?

Productivity, discussed in Chapter 2, is defined as outputs divided by inputs. A global measure of health care output is longevity, but inputs

Exhibit 3.1

	Life Expectancy-Male	*Life Expectancy-Female*	*Health Care Expenditures as a % of GDP*	*Health Care Expenditures Per Capita (in U.S. Dollars)*
Canada	77.2	82.3	8.6	$2,163
China	69.6	72.7	5.5	$49
Germany	75.6	81.6	10.8	$2,412
India	60.1	62.0	5.1	$80
Japan	78.4	85.3	8.0	$2,627
Mexico	71.7	76.9	6.1	$370
Singapore	77.4	81.7	3.9	$816
United Kingdom	75.8	80.5	7.6	$1,835
United States	74.6	79.8	13.9	$4,887

Source: World Health Organization World Health Report, 2001–2004

Note: The figures in this table may differ from those cited elsewhere in the book, as they were computed by the WHO to assure comparability. Data reported elsewhere may use alternative rigorous methods.

can be measured in a variety of ways including the extent of consumer education about health, the number of physicians per capita, the total number of hospital beds, acute illness patient stays and the average length of hospital stays. The summary statistic for all of these inputs is the proportion of GDP or dollar amount per capita spent on health care. Don't make the mistake of assuming that more inputs—dollars, physicians, or anything else—causes better health; it may lead to higher costs but less output if resources are not used efficiently.

The United States spends more and achieves less than most other industrialized nations. Exhibit 3.1 reveals that Canada not only has better overall health, but spends less than half per capita of the United States on health care. Waiting time is reportedly longer for patients to see a physician in Canada, and for elective surgery there are sometimes waiting lists to get on waiting lists, but the price Americans pay for convenience is huge.

Germany, the world's second most expensive health care system (as a percentage of GDP), still spends roughly half per capita as the United States, yet has an average longevity 1.5 years longer than the United States. And although average longevity in Mexico is three years shorter than the United States, it spends only $370 per capita on health care—92 percent less than the United States!

Look at India and China and it becomes obvious these nations are the bargain basements for health care costs. China spends less than $50 per capita on health care, and yet its average longevity differs from the United States by less than a decade. Because the largest health care expenditures occur during the last years of life, one explanation may be that people simply do without. Another conclusion may be that there is a lot of do-it-yourself health care. Regardless, the impact of such dramatically lower health care costs is significant when a U.S. corporation considers establishing a call center or manufacturing plant overseas. And maybe there is something to be learned about how to reduce costs in the United States. People taking responsibility for their own health is a key to increasing productivity of the U.S. health care system and is the basis of consumer driven health care.

There are variations in what is included in health care expenditures for each nation and some quibble that comparisons between nations are never truly "apples to apples." If nations differed only by a few decimal points, such quibbling would probably be justified. But the cost differences between nations are enormous, and while it may be appropriate to examine minor variations due to definitions, the possibility that other industrialized nations are far more productive in their health care systems than the United States cannot be ignored.

How the World Solves the Health Care Problem

Travel around the world and you'll find as many variations in how health care is handled as you'll find variations in when, where, and what people eat. It is no more correct to say that the way health care is practiced in the United States is the "right" way than to say it is "wrong" for Europeans to eat with a fork in their left hand or for Muslims not to eat with their left hand at all. Like any observer of other cultures, our purpose is not to judge, but rather, gather information. For consumer driven health care to work, consumers need information to make good decisions. Other nations may be the source for many of those ideas. Space doesn't permit describing all nations in the same depth and there's no attempt to order or "rank" nations according to most useful in evaluating and reforming the U.S. health care system. A logical starting place is at the U.S. border, the world's longest border between friendly nations, and a line separating nations that share many economic, historical and cultural similarities.

North of the Border: Canada

Canada has a publicly financed health care system, consisting of 13 provincial and territorial health insurance plans supported by the National Health Insurance program (NHI). The Canada Health Act (CHA) establishes criteria for insured health care services that provinces and territories must meet to receive their full allocation of federal funds. The Canadian system assures direct access to medical care for citizens on a prepaid basis with no upfront costs. Five principles underlie the system:

1. Public administration of health care insurance plans on a nonprofit basis.
2. Comprehensive health insurance plans insuring all medically necessary health services. Medically necessary includes hospital fees, physician fees, surgery fees and dental fees.

3. Universal coverage on equal terms and conditions for all insured persons in a province or territory.
4. Portability of insurance for residents that move within the country to different provinces or territories or out of the country.
5. Reasonable access to medically necessary hospital and physician services, regardless of financial or other barriers such as discrimination based on age, race, health status, or other variables.

Government Canada regulates standards for health care through CHA, finances provincial and territorial health care services, and delivers health care services to the military, veterans, Canadian Aboriginals, pensioners, inmates and the Royal Canadian Mounted Police. The federal government also provides education for health promotion and disease prevention.

Provincial and territorial governments manage and deliver insured health services, plan, finance, and evaluate the provision of hospital care and physician and allied health services, and manage prescriptions and public health. Private insurers are forbidden from offering coverage that duplicates the NHI.

In Canada, patients:

1. Do not pay directly for services
2. Do not fill out forms for services at time of service
3. Do not have deductibles
4. Do not have co-pays
5. Do not have dollar limits on coverage for services
6. Receive supplementary health benefits from province or territory governments for:
   a. Prescription drugs
   b. Vision care
   c. Personal medical equipment

Compared to health care in the United States, health care in Canada is more likely to be provided by general practitioners (GPs) who make up 51 percent of all doctors in Canada (1.15 GPs/1000 population). They are the gatekeepers to most other specialists, hospital admissions, diagnostic testing, and prescription drug therapy. Most are private practitioners in independent or group practice, paid on a fee-for-service basis, submitting claims directly to a province/territory health insurance plan. Hospitals, in 95 percent of cases, are operated as private nonprofit entities run by communities, volunteer organizations, or provincial health authorities.

Total health care expenditures are 8.6 percent of GDP with 72.7 percent of funding coming from the public sector and 27.3 percent from the private sector, which includes supplementary insurance, employer-sponsored benefits, and out-of-pocket expenditures by patients. In Canada's government program, the primary sources of funding are:

1. Provincial and federal personal and corporate income taxes
2. Sales taxes, payroll levies, and lottery proceeds in some provinces
3. Alberta and British Columbia use premium payments, but they are not risk-related or a prerequisite for treatment
4. Federal funding transferred to provinces (which must adhere to CHA) as combination of cash contributions and tax transfers

Compared to thousands of third-party insurance companies and state and federal government payers in the United States, Canada achieves administrative efficiencies by a "single payer" system, with the government as the payer. Some studies report administrative overhead as low as 1.3 percent in Canada's NIH versus 31 percent of total health expenditures incurred in the United States.

As Canada's baby boomers' bodies begin to wear out and provincial governments start capping health care expenditures, Canada's health care system is at a crossroads. On the one hand, the government has called for increased emphasis on public health and prevention. On the other hand, the market is ripe for innovators offering home care (due to shortened hospital stays paid by the government system), "cash only" private clinics (which by law cannot accept any government funds), and "outsourcing" of medical care to other nations.

To some degree, the existence of the extensive, but expensive nearby U.S. health care system provides a "back up" for the lower cost Canadian system. Others travel to India or other nations to purchase surgery because the waits for an MRI are too long (six months, according to some reports) and for the surgery. They travel to India because the technology is top-notch and the prices low enough to pay for the airfare, compared to buying the same surgery in the United States.

Many Canadians swear by their health care system, although some swear at it, complaining that private care is illegal except for prisoners and certain government employees. Consumers often complain they must wait too long for treatment or that innovative diagnostic technology is too scarce and too far away. In the United States, physicians complain about increasing demands by HMOs, shrinking discretion over patient care, complex reimbursement procedures, and nonpayment by indigents. In Canada, physicians complain about their low income, scarcity of essential specialties, and the incentive to leave Canada for higher paying positions in other nations, especially one nearby and English-speaking. In spite of its problems, Canada provides quality health care for most of its citizens, and while it costs more than other industrialized nations, it still costs less than the United States.

Hong Kong: Medicine for the Masses

Hong Kong, with an estimated population of seven million, provides medicine for the masses and a substantial proportion of the very wealthy. In 1997, 150 years of British rule ended and Hong Kong became a Special Administrative Region (SAR) of the People's Republic of China. Hong Kong's economic and political philosophy is *laissez faire,* with minimal government regulation and almost all activities, including health care, are left to the market. Still, the Hong Kong SAR provides universal health coverage regardless of financial means.

Hong Kong's total health care expenditures are about 4.6 percent of GDP, 54 percent by public sector and 46 percent by private sector. The public expenditures are financed through general tax revenues (93 percent) and fees and charges (7 percent), such as outpatient and dental charges and charges for licensing drug manufacturers. Patients in public facilities pay a fixed, flat rate for hospital and specialty services. Physicians working in public hospitals and clinics are salaried. The ratio of hospital beds/1000 population is 4.7, with 92 percent of total beds in the public sector and an average occupancy rate of about 83 percent. Major public hospitals also serve as teaching centers and strive to provide the latest technology.

Hong Kong has a ratio of 1.3 physicians/1000 population (compared to 2.7 in the U.S.) and 55 percent are private (mostly general practitioners) with most general practices being solo. Private sector physicians provide 85 percent of ambulatory care and charge a single fee for consultation and medicine dispensing. Drugs are a significant source of income for physicians. In private hospitals, the majority is out-of-pocket household expenditures with the balance coming from privately purchased health insurance and employee benefits.

Hong Kong meets the challenge of large numbers of relatively low paid workers existing alongside many prosperous citizens with three kinds of beds:

1. General ward—$8/day (for people on public assistance, HA hospitals waive all charges)
2. Semiprivate—$75–100/day
3. Private—Maintenance fee/day plus itemized charges

General wards provide a model for how to accommodate large numbers of patients in a cost-effective manner. A ward with many beds achieves greater efficiency in the use of employees and space. Americans are familiar with the large wards of 30 or more beds portrayed in military hospitals. Privacy is nice, but at what cost? In some ways, multiple-bed wards provide better care due to increased patient visibility and monitoring by other patients and their families.

Private hospitals have a shorter wait time, choice of doctor, better amenities, but the same standard of care. They have an occupancy rate of about 35 percent and a median total charge of $1,200 for three days (almost one month's earnings of the typical fully employed worker.)

Although Hong Kong is effective at assuring a base level of care with both public and private providers, the system is not without problems. The quality of care is perceived to be highly variable, possibly due to self-regulation of the medical profession without interference from external organizations (*laissez faire*). The health care system is highly compartmentalized with a lack of coordination, and some question its long-term financial sustainability, believing it may lack capacity, competency, and information to be efficient in the future. In this mixture between primary and inpatient care and private and public sectors, services get duplicated; there is sometimes discontinuity of care and a frequent complaint is that patients are confused about their care. Nevertheless, it is a system which provides low cost health care of reasonable, although variable, quality for the masses simultaneously with high quality health care for those who can afford the private system.

> *Solution to America's "Two Trillion Dollar Crisis": Good quality health care for patients without insurance coverage or private funds could be provided at lower cost with large, multiple-bed wards.*

Europe: "You're Covered"

Although each member country of the European Union has some variation of socialized medicine, most provide a model of universal coverage funded by a combination of tax dollars and user premiums, and administered by a mixture of public and private insurance carriers and health care providers. As a result, the most frequent answer Europeans receive when they need access to health care is, "You're covered."

An examination of the health care system in Germany provides insight as to how the European Model works. The Social Code Book of Germany is the principal legislation that requires all people to be insured under some statutory health insurance (SHI) scheme. SHI covers 88 percent of the population (74 percent mandatory and 14 percent voluntary members and dependents). High income earners can opt out of SHI and purchase private health insurance, as does about nine percent of the population. Germany is the largest voluntary health insurance (VHI) market in Europe with 52 private health insurers. Free governmental health insurance is provided to about two percent of the population, including police, military, civil service employees and those on social welfare. Less than 0.2 percent is uninsured.

Funding of the German health care system is achieved primarily through social health insurance contributions, based on income. The average contribution rate is 14 percent, shared equally by employers and employees. For patients in SHI, purchases and payments are made from 420 "sickness" funds (337 company-based). Traditionally, most people have not had a choice of fund, but were assigned to a fund based on location and job—however, the Health Care Structure Act of 1996 gave almost everyone a right to choose, change, or cancel sickness funds freely. In many other European nations, citizens cannot choose their insurer, but are automatically affiliated with an insurer based on location and job.

After the United States, Germany is the second most expensive health care system in the world, consuming about 11 percent of GDP (75 percent public, of which 8.4 percent is by taxes, and 25 percent private). There is no "gatekeeper" system to see a specialist and patients can select their own physician. Ambulatory care and hospital care are totally distinct with no outpatient care in a mix of public and private hospitals designed to be efficient rather than. Hospital admission requires referral from ambulatory-setting physicians, except in emergencies. Ambulatory care is provided by private, office-based physicians, both generalists and specialists, paid on a fee-for-service basis. Given the strict separation between ambulatory and hospital care, it is not surprising that a common complaint among Germans is a lack of continuity and transition.

Although nearly everyone is covered in Germany, there are co-pays for government-insured patients, about $12 per day for the first 14 days in a hospital, $17/trip for ambulance transport, and 15 percent of nonphysician care. Many other European nations have co-pays on physician visits, prescription drugs, lab tests, and other services. In Germany, there is no co-pay for ambulatory care, preventive dental care, low income patients, the unemployed, those on social welfare, and children under 18 years. The annual out-of-pocket limit is two percent of gross income and chronically ill patients that have paid one percent of gross income are exempt. Also, all out-of-pocket health care expenditures are tax-deductible.

Privately insured patients in Germany must pay health care providers directly (fee-for-service) and then get reimbursed by the insurer. The real fee-for-service reimbursement has led to cost increases which are about 40 percent higher than for people covered by SHI. This is different from SHI payments in which physicians are paid by capitation, a flat fee based on the number of members in a group. Physician reimbursement is controlled to prevent over-utilization or false claims. Physicians are paid by fees-for-service only for privately insured patients. Hospital payments in Germany are based on investment costs, "running" (operational) costs, reimbursed through prospective case fees and procedural fees as well as per diem fees. The Reform Act of Statutory Health Insurance of 2000 mandated hospital payments based on diagnostic related group (DRGs) for all patients.

In Europe, coverage is often rigidly defined, but fairly comprehensive and efficient. Before anyone jumps to the conclusion that the

European system seems ideal, they should also understand the problems. The pervasive difficulty in readily obtaining health care has led citizens to demand Patient's Rights legislation. There is also a shortage of doctors, due to both a ceiling on doctors' fees and medical school enrollment quotas. Chronic discontent with the relatively low income levels of health care professionals sometimes leads to "strikes"—in which patients are told that health care will not be available until the strike is settled.

Despite the widespread coverage, there is still a tradition for many families to look first to themselves for remedies for ordinary illnesses. In both the pharmacies of Europe and in the pocketbooks of many grandmothers are found herbal remedies that consumers have turned to for centuries. Arnica, a white flower known to reduce inflammation and decrease pain by stimulating the activity of white blood cells, is as common across Europe as aspirin is in the United States. One of the reasons health care costs are lower may be the tendency to look first to oneself, to the "chemist" or pharmacist, or to Grandmother before calling the doctor, even though they're covered by insurance when they do. That's important to consider in a consumer driven health care with a Health Savings Account in which to accumulate funds for consumers who save money by handling routine health needs on a DIY basis.

India: Land of the Future

The two eye-popping statistics that may have caught your attention in Exhibit 3.1 are the amounts spent on health care in India and China. With more than a billion people each, both countries are challenged with how to keep so many people working and healthy, but these questions are closely related. If you are also concerned about how to keep people working in advanced industrialized economies such as the United States, it is important to understand how health care works in China and India because their lower health care costs give both countries a decisive edge in labor costs over the United States. At nearly $7,000, the cost of health insurance for a typical U.S. worker is greater than the average annual salary in many of the world's most competitive nations!

Since India has attracted so much media attention as an attractive place to outsource technology and other white-collar jobs, let's take a look at Indian health care and why at $80 per capita and 5.1 percent of GDP, its costs are so much lower than in the United States. The basic reason why health care costs are so low in India is that most people can't afford to pay more. Health insurance has only a small foothold in India, even though insurance is common for life, home, and automobile. As a consequence, most people still pay cash for their health care, making many of the indirect costs inherent in the U.S. system almost nonexistent in India. Health care costs are under the control of a family's microeconomic budget. If medicine is needed to treat an illness, Indian consumers look for the cheapest solution in order to save money for other necessities such as rice and milk. If an Indian consumer is unable to pay $10 for a pill, then the pharmaceutical company cannot sell that pill. Companies must manufacture for less cost and accept lower prices. If consumers have a cold or fever, they have a choice of a doctor who might charge the U.S. equivalent of $50 per visit plus insurance charges or an alternative care physician who charges the U.S. equivalent of $5 per visit, paid out of pocket by the patient. If both are believed to bring the same results, which would you choose? In India, people seem to harness the concept of self-medication more than in the United States partly due to the fact that they can't afford to do anything else. The U.S. system of depending on insurance companies to pay for health care creates a type of blindness. If American consumers had to pay the full costs out of pocket, it is quite possible they too would look for cheaper solutions to America's "Two Trillion Dollar Crisis."

The India Department of Health and Family Welfare regulates fees, licenses hospitals and maintains other services including the Department of Indian Systems of Medicine and Homoeopathy (ISM&H), which promotes education, sets standards for medicinal plants and therapeutic Yoga, conducts efficacy tests and communicates information about traditional Indian forms of health care.

In the conventional allopathic approach followed in much of the West, pharmaceuticals are prescribed to treat diseases and their symptoms. Two alternatives to allopathy are popular in India. In the homeopathic approach, the symptoms of an illness are viewed as a direct manifestation of the body's attempt to heal itself and a homeopathic substance is given to stimulate the body's own natural healing capacity. Homeopathy was "discovered" more than 200 years ago by the German researcher Dr. Christian Friedrich Samuel Hahnemann, although its practice spans back to ancient times. While more than

2,000 remedies have been investigated, most diseases are treated by less than 100 of them, allowing practitioners to familiarize themselves readily with the effects. Another form of alternative medicine is Ayurveda, or herbal medicine. Some Americans may not be aware that "gardener" is an important job title in many hospitals around the world that believe low cost natural remedies are just as effective for everyday illnesses as modern pharmaceuticals.

India's lack of trained medical practitioners has spawned government-sponsored programs that provide health training for selected persons of several villages. Monthly meetings of village health workers are held to discuss health care issues in their areas, and teach basic techniques of physical exercise, Yoga, disease control and other health-promoting activities. While these services are operated primarily in remote village and tribal areas where medical facilities are limited, people have responded enthusiastically and similar projects are slated for other states. Just as important as the type of medicine practiced, is the concept that people can be instructed and motivated to affect their own health by their own activities.

> *Solution to America's "Two Trillion Dollar Crisis": U.S. health authorities should analyze the research and experience with alternative medicines and self-medication to determine which are less expensive and/or more efficacious than those in the United States.*

Other factors lower costs in India. Most medical care is still delivered by a general practitioner within the first or second visit and referrals are rare. In the United States, many insurance companies ask that a patient first see a "gatekeeper" before seeing a specialist regardless of the illness, incurring the costs of multiple consultations. This is partly due to malpractice litigation and the need for physicians and insurers to follow proper procedures to protect themselves from blame, consumers lacking knowledge to select health care providers, and the need for multiple tests to "prove the diagnosis" to the insurance company.

Is it really less cost efficient for informed consumers to see specialists directly instead of first consulting a "gatekeeper"? That's a question begging for more research and one that's now causing some HMOs and insurers to revise their policies to encourage consumers to bypass the gatekeepers. But in India, where consumers pay from their own pockets, the incentive to find the most effective and lowest cost provider is much greater than the third-party payer system of the United States.

The business costs for health care practice are also much lower in India not only due to lower labor costs, but also because much of the paperwork that nurses and administrative staff perform in the United States is not necessary in a system based on consumers paying their own bills in cash. Rarely do patients go to a doctor's office in India and find an expensive professional building with air conditioned offices and reserved parking spaces. The typical health care business is a "no frills" operation managed to keep costs low while still running an effective practice.

Solution to America's "Two Trillion Dollar Crisis": Analyze and adopt a process that costs less when patients pay for health care services and medicines from their own funds instead of billing someone else.

There is also little to no malpractice litigation in India, thus eliminating the litigation and malpractice insurance costs of health care. When U.S. doctors purchase malpractice insurance of $50,000 to $100,000 or more per year, there is no alternative except to pass the cost on to patients. In contrast to the United States, where people tend to want someone to blame for every unfortunate outcome, doctors in India have little pressure to practice "defensive medicine"—over-testing, over-diagnosing, and over-prescribing to protect themselves from a malpractice lawsuit. If there is a tragic outcome, the culture gives the doctors the benefit of the doubt, insisting they did their best and that there was no mal-intent.

Solution to America's "Two Trillion Dollar Crisis": Analyze whether malpractice suits should be based on mal-practice or mal-intent.

While it is important to recognize that alternative medicine and self-treatment is important in understanding India's lower costs, one should not jump to the conclusion that India lacks technology. The difference is that technology in India is not the major driving force of health care cost that it is in the United States. India is known for its leadership in software development and network operations, causing firms to transfer a greater portion of their routine tasks such as application maintenance and data processing. Rather than spending copious amounts of dollars on technological research, India adopts technology proven successful in other nations, leaving many research costs in the shadows.

Fortunately, India and the rest of the world still looks to the United States for innovation and the future of the U.S. economy will depend on the ability of American companies, universities, and government institutions to provide marketable solutions to the world's problems. But what happens when people want their insurance companies to pay for the newest and most expensive "cures," resulting in increased health care costs due to technology? And what happens when such resulting health care expenditures make the United States unable to sell its innovation abroad? In consumer driven health care, market forces will reveal new ways to pay for the medical innovation and scientific advancements that keep America on the forefront of the global economy, while still making health care affordable.

Medical Tourism

The trend to outsource computer and other technology talent to India is also occurring in health care services, spawning a new industry known as "medical tourism." Consumers increasingly travel to China, India, the Caribbean, South Africa, and other destinations for dental work, cosmetic surgery, or other treatments—enjoying luxury accommodations, first class travel, and some of the world's greatest scenery—all for less than the price of comparable services in the United States (including airfare).

Entrepreneurs worldwide have jumped on this phenomenon. *The Wall Street Journal* (April 26, 2004) describes the practice of Dr. Prathap C. Reddy, 72, an American-trained physician who founded Apollo Hospital and now runs it with his four daughters in Madras (also known as Chennai), India. Apollo performs health care services so well and at such lower costs that it attracts patients from high-priced nations. Typical is Terry Salo, who flew 22 hours from his home in Victoria, British Columbia for a partial hip replacement at Apollo. Salo, a former commercial fisherman, faced a wait of a year or more for free care from Canada's National Health Service but the pain had become unbearable. Before airfare and other expenses, he paid $4,500 for the surgery at Apollo Hospitals, a quarter of the cost for similar treatment in Europe and the United States. "People need to know that there are other options out there," says Mr. Salo, 54 years old, who was swinging golf clubs a month after the operation. Salo is one of 60,000 foreign patients who were treated at Apollo Hospitals over the past three years. Since its start as a single hospital in 1983, Apollo has grown to 37 hospitals with more than 6,400 beds, making it one of the largest private hospital chains in Asia. Apollo's emergence as a global health-care provider in many ways tracks India's economic trajectory over the past three decades. The company has capitalized on the high cost of health care administration in the United States and demands of patients elsewhere for fast, inexpensive but high-quality treatment.

Medical tourism isn't always based on finding the lowest price. The United Arab Emirates is currently building a self-contained "Medical City" in Dubai, which it hopes will attract an array of international specialists catering to the very wealthy. This super-modern facility will integrate world-class treatment with cutting-edge technology. Through an alliance with Scotland's prestigious University of Edinburgh, medical students from around the world will be able to learn alongside the world's best physicians. And true to Dubai, patients and their families will enjoy the highest quality of care in ultra-posh "Disneyland-like" surroundings.

> *Solution to America's "Two Trillion Dollar Crisis": Reduce the cost of health care in the United States by purchasing some procedures from nations with lower costs and/or more advanced procedures. Institutions in the United States may also learn how to improve their own efficiency by studying some of the most efficient in lower-cost nations.*

Singapore

No crime. No poverty. No dirt. And the best health care in the world. Welcome to Singapore. If you read one of its newspapers, jog on its streets, walk through its hospitals, or talk to its citizens about their health care, as we have done, you may conclude that these phrases are all nearly all true. Less than 40 years ago, Singapore was an impoverished, exploited colony with famine, disease, illiteracy, and poverty. Today its 4.2 million citizens find themselves in comfortable apartments with jobs, clean streets, and affordable, readily accessible health care. Singapore's labor productivity exceeds all nations including the United States, its freeways are designed never to be clogged with traffic, its airline consistently wins awards for customer service and profitability, its logistics facilities create the most efficient port in the world, the education of its professors and physicians are the best financed in the world, and even the restrooms at the super-efficient Changi airport are so clean, carpeted and odor-free that you could almost enjoy lunch in them. (For a brief description of these achievements, see Chapter 10 in *From the Edge of the World*, OSU Press, 1995).

A recent study by Canadian health care economist Cynthia Ramsay used an index (ranging from zero to 100) similar to the United Nations Human Development Index and the Fraser Institute Index of Human Progress to compare the relative performance of health care systems. "Quality" is measured using such categories as health status, mortality rates, preventable illnesses, appropriateness of services and patient satisfaction. "Access to care" measures insurance coverage in a population, equity in health outcomes, how health spending is distributed between acute and other health care services, and the availability of medical expertise and technology. "Cost" variables include efficiency and total health spending, and sustainability. Based on these variables, Singapore has the worlds "best" health care system with a score of 62.1. By contrast, the United States ranked fourth with a score of 53.6. Obviously, the United States has something to learn from Singapore, especially considering that Singapore spends only 3.9 percent of GDP on health care, or $816 per person with a government subsidy of only one percent in 2002, yet the average life expectancy rate is 77.4 years for men and 81.7 years for women. Rising standards of living, high standards of education, good housing, sanitation, a high level of medical services, and the active promotion of preventive medicine have all helped significantly to give Singapore one of the best records for health in the world.

James C. Collins and Jerry I. Porrous in the best-selling business book of the last decade, *Built to Last* (HarperBusiness, 1994), describe how mission and strategy are critical to the most successful organizations in the world. Health care in Singapore is overseen by the Ministry of Health, whose mission is *to promote good health and reduce illness*, and whose strategy involves the following philosophies/practices:

- Good health is to a great extent the responsibility of the individual
- The Ministry plays a major role in educating and providing information to the public on how they can maintain good healthy lifestyles
- The Ministry also plays a key role in reducing illness in Singapore through the control and prevention of diseases and ensuring that the resources are allocated appropriately to do this

This strategy is implemented with insurance plans based on individual responsibility and government subsidies. The government not only encourages, but requires all employed people to set aside six to eight percent of their income into a Medisave account to pay for their own health care costs. Additional programs include Medishield, which provides for catastrophic illness, and Medifund, which provides for indigent consumers and achieves universal coverage for Singapore.

You can see a lot of the features of consumer driven health care when observing Singapore. Singapore is a health care system based on patient choices, in which consumers:

1. Are free to choose providers
2. Can walk into any private clinic or any government polyclinic and receive care
3. Can go to an emergency room 24 hours/day
4. Benefit from an emphasis on preventive care

The government program excludes nonessential cosmetic services, experimental drugs, and unproven procedures, but is tied together, since 1999, into two (public and private) vertically integrated delivery networks.

The core reason why the Singapore health care system is so successful is that it avoids "free care" by requiring co-pays for ordinary doctor visits, which increase with the cost of care. For consumers choosing lower classes (but not lower quality) of care including public hospital wards, the government subsidizes about 80 percent of the costs. This assures nobody does without, but also provides an incentive to be healthy, save money and choose wisely. The market drives efficiency in the delivery of health care but the government insures the market works efficiently.

The Ministry of Health is responsible for ensuring that health care is characterized by good clinical outcomes and professional standards, and that services delivered are appropriate to each patient's needs. Although the Ministry of Health emphasizes the principle of co-payment, it also ensures that health care remains affordable. One of the ways this is accomplished is a website where consumers can instantly view the 50th and 90th percentile prices for every procedure and service in every hospital. If you visit the Singapore Ministry of Health website (*www.moh.gov.sg*), you'll find one of the best-designed, easiest-to-use, and most helpful websites in the world. Among other things, it provides complete web-based applications, reports on health care providers, information on Traditional Chinese Medicine, Severe Acute Respiratory Syndrome (SARS) and other ailments, healthy lifestyles, and current health-related news. Other topics include ElderCare, Singapore's innovative program to provide services to the elderly that help people stay in their homes, moving to institutional facilities only as a last resort, and ElderShield, an affordable severe disability insurance scheme designed to provide basic financial protection in the event of severe disabilities. If you read the annual reports of the Ministry of Health, you'll also discover that part of the success of Singapore includes employer-based programs to implement daily exercise, promote consumption of fruits and vegetables and celebrate those who live healthily and reduce health care costs.

The most important lesson to be applied to the U.S. health care system is efficiency, driven by consumers in charge of their own health. When consumers are in control, they evaluate their options and choose the lowest cost, most efficient providers. For example, compare inpatient surgery rates between the United States and Singapore. In the United States, many third-party payers (including the government) will not reimburse a physician for services provided on an outpatient basis when the third-party payer "requires" a hospital stay. Also, a physician may be hesitant to release someone from the hospital, lest he be held legally liable for anything that should happen. As a result, the United States has the world's highest inpatient surgery rate at 87.4 (per 1,000 population) compared to Singapore's rate of 45.3. Singapore, by contrast, relies more on cost-effective outpatient or "day surgery."

When patients do require a hospital stay, Singapore is more efficient at utilizing hospital beds with an occupancy rate of 74.1 percent compared to the United States at 63.9 percent. The high-tech, good-health, market-driven health care system of Singapore also yields shorter hospital stays, averaging 4.8 days versus 6.2 days in the United States.

As a result of its efficiency, Singapore is able to deliver its excellent level of health care with less than half the number of physicians per capita as the United States. It is a major advantage to be a small nation with a high-tech, education-oriented value system, but think of how health care costs would be affected if major U.S. cities adopted the same methods and values.

Talk to consumers who use and depend on the Singapore health care system and you'll generally find a high level of satisfaction with a system in which they can generally expect:

1. Treatment will be good and up-to-date
2. Treatment will be cost-effective and of proven value
3. Not the latest and best of everything
4. No frills, but an integrated supply chain of high quality services and medicines

No system is a utopia, of course, and Singapore has its problems, including rising costs for technology and innovation, rising expectations, and a shortage of nurses and paramedics. Singapore's population is also rapidly aging. The percentage of the population over age 60 will increase from 11 to 27 percent by 2030, which will put more stress on health care funding.

The key to Singapore's success is consumers spending their own money, the rationale for consumer driven health care. The government requires them to save money for health care, allows them to choose where their health care savings will be used, provides education and information to help them make informed choices, and regulates the quantity and quality of providers from which consumers choose.

> *Solution to America's "Two Trillion Dollar Crisis":*
> *A national board representing reform of the U.S. health care system should begin by analyzing and adopting the best features of the Singapore health care system.*

Who's Right?

It is difficult to look at the health care systems of any nation without placing them into the context of that nation's political economy. Should the government fund and operate the health care system or should it be done by consumers in a market-driven economy? To understand the realities of the American health care system, it is useful to remember that the United States was founded for marketing purposes, populated and governed mostly by marketers, and financed by marketing (trading) corporations principally from England and to a lesser extent from Holland. The best selling book, *Freedom Just Around the Corner* by historian Walter McDougall (HarperCollins, 2004) describes how the market-driven system underlies America's economic system, in contrast to the state-controlled systems of other countries. That's important to remember when comparing the U.S. health care system with those of other nations. Changing from a market-driven health care system to a government-controlled health care system would be counter to the culture and constitution of the United States and about as likely to be adopted as changing the U.S. electoral system to the parliamentary system. Because we are a market-driven system, the solutions to our problems will be driven by how well those who want to fix health care costs understand markets, marketing and consumer behavior. Thus, consumer driven health care is truly a marketing solution to America's "Two Trillion Dollar Crisis."

CHAPTER 4

The Crisis of Indirect Health Care Costs

*"If you take a dog which is starving and feed him
and make him prosperous, that dog will not bite you.
This is the primary difference between a dog and a man."*
—Mark Twain (1835–1910)

If you are already alarmed by the size of America's "Two Trillion Dollar Crisis," you may weep when you realize that more than 60 percent of the cost involves no health *care* at all. Instead, funds go to transferring most financial and many medical decisions to large outside bureaucracies, recording and storing patient data (often repeatedly for the same patient), operating hospitals with 36 percent of the beds unused and so inefficient that both patients and physicians spend much of their time waiting, enduring unnecessary procedures and sacrificing millions to defend against malpractice, and paying 10 percent of total costs for fraudulent claims. All are part of the "overhead" or what is called the indirect costs of health care.

Who Suffers: Patients or Payers?

If you have a pet, you probably receive postcards from your neighborhood veterinarian several times a year reminding you of scheduled vaccines and examinations. When you call for an appointment, typically you can get in right away (even on a Saturday), the staff is most likely friendly and not only takes time to explain your pet's condition, but also gives you a number of choices for your pet's treatment. Not only can you fill any prescriptions on the spot, if you plan ahead, the animal hospital may even provide a bath, dental cleaning, or spa treatment, and your furry friend will always receive a treat at the end of the visit. Why? It's because you pay cash.

For your own health care, you'll likely wait until pain disrupts your daily life to call the doctor's office and then wait several weeks for an appointment, scheduled at a time and location convenient to the physician (meaning you'll have to miss work or other activities). In the office, you'll complete several forms (many requiring the same information) wait until an examination room is ready and then again to see a nurse and physician. You'll get limited time with the medical staff and limited choice of treatments, and you'll have to "fight" to get anything out of the ordinary. Afterwards, you'll spend hours filling prescriptions, tracking claims, and paying bills. Is the difference that physicians don't care about people the way veterinarians care about pets? No—it's that physicians don't work for you! They work for whoever pays the bills. When the payer is a large insurance company, HMO or the federal government, health care providers do what those entities are willing to approve and reimburse.

In the 1960s, the United States spent only about five percent of GDP on health care, of which 55 percent was paid by consumers, costing $144 per capita or $76 out-of-pocket. Between 1960 and 2000, overall health costs increased 4,800 percent and the percentage paid by "someone else" (other than out-of-pocket by consumers) soared to 82.8 percent, as illustrated by Exhibit 4.1. Today, health care expenditures constitute more than 15 percent of GDP and consumers pay 17 percent of the total, or $700 per year, yet studies show the average American spends less than five minutes per year consulting with a physician. A distant third-party payer now has ownership of the health care system and expects both health care providers and consumers to conform to its needs, which include accepting the diagnoses and treatments it agrees to reimburse, at locations or with "preferred" business partners it designates, and at prices it has negotiated in advance. To administer such a massive bureaucracy that approves and reimburses medical expenditures, third-party payers must have a way to monitor the patient-provider relationship. Contracts are the mechanism and enforcement is by paperwork.

Drowning in a Sea of Paper

The paperwork burden of health care takes caregivers away from patient bedsides at staggering levels of cost. In a care setting like an emergency room, there is one hour of paperwork for every hour of patient care; and in surgery and acute patient care, there are 36 min-

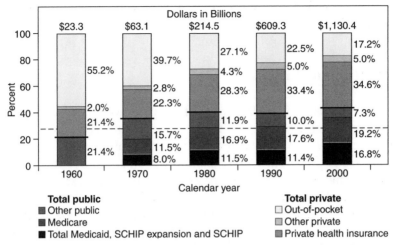

Exhibit 4.1   Personal Health Care Expenditures by Source of Funds:
Selected Years 1960–2000

utes of paperwork for every hour of patient care, as illustrated in
Exhibit 4.2.

Because there are so many payers, each with different regulations,
payment rules, technology, and reimbursement methods, the average
U.S. hospital can spend 25 percent of its budget on billing and administration without evidence that it improves patient care. Overall,
this fragmented and broken system of charging, billing and collection
consumes about 31 cents of every health care dollar. In a single-payer
system where all bills are sent to one agency (as in Canada), administrative costs run as low as one or two percent. When patients are responsible for their own medical bills (paid through their HSAs), the

Exhibit 4.2

Type of Treatment	Amount of time health care providers spend on paperwork, per hour of direct patient care
Emergency Room	60 Minutes
Surgery and Acute Patient Care (Inpatient)	36 Minutes
Skilled Nursing Care	30 Minutes
Home Health Care	48 Minutes

paperwork burden of routine health care will be significantly reduced, saving as much as $140 billion annually.

An Inefficient Process

Consider the case of an 80-year-old patient, who after several days of symptoms is referred directly to the local hospital emergency room (ER) because her Medicare-paid physician's office schedule is full. She arrives in the ER at 11:00 A.M. and within an hour, a triage nurse begins taking her medical history. After another hour, she is referred to X-Ray, and after yet another hour is seen by a physician, along with two other people again collecting her medical history. Because hospital discharges are often slow and inefficient, it's 3:00 P.M. before she is assigned to a hospital bed, and the process repeats with a variety of nurses, transfer personnel, assistants, X-ray technicians, staff physicians, interns, residents, and finally an attending surgeon. The patient is ready for gall bladder surgery at 11:00 P.M. During this 12–hour preparation, 11 different people take her medical history, asking nearly identical questions, with varying attention to detail and almost no reference to each other's notes. One medical history per hour: at least the hospital is diligent! A couple of days later, the patient is discharged, a process that involves a six-hour wait for family members who again complete various forms. Weeks later, the patient, now recovering at home, receives separate bills from a dozen different service providers, without any explanation as to what is reimbursable, what has been submitted to Medicare for reimbursement, what is payable by secondary policies, or even how the charges were determined. As a result, the billing statements and "past due" notices begin collecting in a kitchen drawer.

If software developers can create powerful search engines like Google and Yahoo! and industry leaders can agree on a Uniform Product Code (UPC) to identify every conceivable product in the world, why isn't there an IT solution to collect, store, and disseminate patient medical and billing data? Although it's logical to infer that an information-based field like health care would invest heavily in IT, the actual percentage of total budget spent on health care IT is only two percent, compared to other industries like financial services which spend more than 10 percent. In fact, 80 percent of hospitals and 95 percent of doctor's offices use the same methods for storing and accessing patient data as they did 50 years ago, mostly paper and film stuffed in huge metal cabinets.

Entering and retrieving information using paper-based medical records consumes up to 38 percent of the physician's time, which explains why 60 percent of hospitals are either currently installing or planning to install electronic medical records. For example, Catholic Hospital West of San Francisco is investing $137 million in an eight-year IT initiative to improve patient safety, integrating radiology films and reports, the pharmacy, the laboratory, intensive care, and emergency departments. The information system will support physician order entry, clinical physician support, and computerized drug rules to prevent adverse drug events, and interfaces with the patient at the bedside. Other solutions include a comprehensive data warehouse of patient records, with industry standards of care, quality benchmarks, and disease management protocols built into decision-making systems.

At the Ohio State University, the "One-Chart" program allows transplant patients to access their own medical records and update their own medical data (including the results of laboratory tests) over the telephone or Internet. Productivity has increased, reducing the time transplant coordinators have to spend on the phone by 50 percent and allowing six doctors and seven nurses to manage as many as 4,000 transplant patients. More important, the transplant database has improved patient care by reducing admissions to the hospital for postsurgical complications and rates of rejection of the transplant.

Clinical mistakes, which account for 75,000 to 100,000 deaths in the United States each year, could be reduced by information technology. When fully implemented in health care systems, physician offices and individual hospitals, information sharing systems are estimated to save nearly $87 billion a year.

Everything's Up to Date in Bundang

If you want to see the world's first fully digitalized hospital, follow a star in the East to South Korea's Seoul National University Bundang Hospital. Opened in May 2004 as a 550–bed facility with 23 medical departments treating 1,500 outpatients daily, Bundang offers advanced services including mammography, ultrasound, magnetic resonance imaging, cardiac angiography, nuclear imaging, and a range of image-guided interventions. All medical information including x-rays, diagnosed conditions, allergies and drug interactions are stored on each patient's magnetic card, which is read by a machine similar to an ATM or airline kiosk. Readers are strategically placed throughout the hospital, providing physicians and nurses unprecedented information about a patient and his medical history, all within seconds of patient contact. It's not just information for admissions, imaging, billing, or lab tests; the system automates everything needed to improve health *care* and lower costs, in every area of the hospital. IT and people—together they are the keys to reducing indirect costs. The only paper you'll find in Bundang Hospital is in the restroom.

A "Hi-Fi" Solution

Radio Frequency Identification (RFID) is rapidly increasing efficiency of retail stores by placing "chips" on cases and pallets that allow firms such as Gillette and Wal-Mart to monitor products moving over the road, into warehouses, and out to stores. When individual items are RFID-enabled, consumers will be able to bypass the traditional "cashier" and push their carts through a self-service "antenna" which immediately identifies and tallies each item. Eliminating cashiers will save billions of dollars in labor and benefits expense and hours of time for consumers. The paper problem in health care can be likewise addressed with individual patient identification tags. A tiny RFID chip fastened onto a hospital bracelet could allow a nurse or physician to pull up a patient's up-to-date medical records the moment they enter a room.

Consumers can drive technology by demanding online access to their medical data. Until recently consumers have been completely blind as to their medical records, despite having the biggest stake in assuring its accuracy. Medical information such as blood type and drug allergies embedded digitally on a consumer's driver's license or ID card could be life-saving when emergency vehicles and ERs are equipped with readers that provide an immediate history to health care personnel.

In a hospital or physician's office, a smart card containing a patient's personal medical profile could be scanned, transmitting data instantly to third-party payers for approval. Technologically-advanced call centers could verify and approve payment and set an appointment with a specialist—all within minutes. Patient information could then be shared with supply chain partners to assure personnel and supplies were in place to administer treatment. Not only would billions of dollars be saved by reducing paper records stacking up in hospital and physician storerooms, redundant lab tests, and repeated questions from hospital personnel, it would also produce happier patients and save some lives.

Acceptance of IT solutions requires universally recognized and uniform standards for documenting and transmitting health care data. Billing data formats are feasible to develop, with languages such as XML that enable communication between data sets already available. There's progress on a standard core vocabulary and syntax of clinical terminology allowing collection and processing of comparable clinical data from diverse medical sectors without the biases that arise from clinical terms used in different disciplines.

> *Solution to America's "Two Trillion Dollar Crisis": A national standards group should be convened to determine specifications for personal medical profiles that can be used by all medical institutions, accessed and maintained by individual consumers.*

Privacy and Payment

Federal regulation over the confidentiality of patient data creates a barrier to obtaining and analyzing clinical information needed to treat patients effectively and for health care markets to operate efficiently across providers. Increasing awareness that the inaccessible and fragmented nature of health care information may harm patients has strengthened attempts to create a single, comprehensive, readily accessible medical record. However, unlike data repositories developed for and by providers, insurance companies, and analysts, the best solution is for data to be owned and controlled by patients themselves. This could be accomplished with an integrated system of personal health profiles that follow universal standards and contain each individual's complete, up-to-date medical history, perhaps carried on a wallet-sized card.

A major obstruction is HIPPA, the Federal Health Insurance Portability and Privacy Act, passed in 1996 and implemented in

2002–2003. When patients go to a physician's office or seek admission to a hospital, they are always asked to read and sign a statement that "the results of any diagnosis or test will be confided only to the patient, unless expressed, written permission is provided for a third-party to access the information." Although HIPPA was intended to end the practice by insurance companies of "cherry picking" or denying coverage to those with chronic or preexisting conditions, the unintended consequence may have been to discourage adoption of innovative IT solutions by threatening legal action if privacy is perceived to be unprotected. HIPPA consumes tons of paper and hours of patient and staff time. Perhaps it even reduces patient information and privacy compared to a less onerous and threatening process to inform patients and encourage them to understand and use their personal medical data.

Once educated about the importance and the reality of lowering costs in consumer driven health care, consumers should be willing to share health data with information intermediaries, provided their privacy will be protected. Motivation can come from financial incentives or a need for easy access to complete personal health records. Impossible to accomplish, some say, but it was also said that consumers would never provide their credit card information to Internet sellers! Over time, consumers identify and differentiate firms that earn their trust (those with secure websites), and those that do not. The same will happen in a consumer driven health care environment when consumers understand and benefit from adopting new information technologies.

Using Resources Efficiently

In physicians' offices and hospitals, the "waiting room" is aptly named. How much does it cost for an employee to miss a half-day of work sitting in the doctor's office with a sick child? If the opportunity costs of lost productivity are included, total health care costs would exceed even 15 percent of GDP. Ironically, as patients wait, existing facilities sit partially empty, and massive additional costs are being sunk into new construction.

When a need existed in a city of one million residents for a new heart hospital to lower costs, improve efficiency, and provide specialized services, the area's leading academic hospital estimated the cost at $45 million. However, after it announced its plans, two competing local hospitals decided they too wanted new heart hospitals, resulting in three facilities adding a total of $170 million of capital expenditures to health care costs with little improvement in overall care. Today, all three are operating well below capacity, bleeding red ink, and battling each other with TV and billboard ads proclaiming "we're the best" and "we care more about your heart." Efficiency—in terms of surgical outcomes and costs—is less than what could have been accomplished for $45 million. No major hospital wants to be left behind, but rather, wishes to be all things to all people with others—employers, insurance companies, charitable foundations, and the government—paying the bill. When medical institutions are fighting for all-or-nothing contracts with HMOs, it's important they be able to offer an array of services, instead of concentrating on the things they can do most effectively and efficiently. In consumer driven health care, however, consumers will migrate towards the highest quality, lowest cost providers, encouraging the grouping of specialties to create economies of scale and attract and leverage the most qualified talent.

Proven Processes to Improve Efficiency

Can we really improve efficiency in health care? Sometimes the solution is as simple as physicians changing when they issue discharge orders. When issued in the morning, discharge often occurs so late in the day that the bed is unused that night. However, writing orders in the afternoon of the day before expected discharge (which can be changed if necessary the following day), allows patients to be discharged on a more orderly schedule, opening the bed for use the following evening.

U.S. manufacturers attacked inefficiency years ago with dramatic results, a good indication that the same can be accomplished in health care delivery. For example, Dell Computer recently implemented a company-wide initiative designed to triple output with one-half the number of workers. If similar initiatives could be deployed in hospitals, physician offices, and insurance companies, the indirect costs of health care could be reduced by half, saving $800 billion and reducing the proportion of U.S. GDP devoted to health care to levels equaling those of other industrialized nations. Not only would this release funds for improved patient care—the direct costs of health care—patients would also be more satisfied with the health care they receive.

Effective Marketing: The Key to Providing More Efficient Health Care

Casual observers sometimes confuse marketing with selling. Simply stated, selling is getting people to buy what an organization produces, but marketing is producing what consumers will buy, at a price high enough to cover costs. Marketing, fundamentally, is creating or changing organizations to produce what consumers will buy at prices they are willing to pay.

Whether the "product" is health care delivery, financial services, or anything else, certain inescapable business activities are required to get goods from producer to consumer. Although their names may vary, these universal marketing functions always include exchange (buying and selling), physical distribution (transporting and storing), and facilitating (standardizing, financing, risk taking and securing marketing information). These functions must be completed in order to perform the *production* functions—delivering health care, described in the next chapter as *direct* costs of the health care system. Enduring success in any industry occurs by performing marketing functions more efficiently and serving customers better than competitors.

The key to efficiency is to shift marketing "functions" to the most efficient channel member. That may be a manufacturer (such as pharmaceutical or medical device manufacturer), wholesaler (such as Cardinal Health or McKesson HBOC), retailer (such as a hospital or physician), specialized agency (insurance company, IT supplier, or management firm) or customers (patients and their families in consumer driven health care). Many people think Nike is a manufacturer but it is actually a distributor and, to a lesser extent, a retailer. Because of Nike's superior capabilities in branding and supply chain management, it is best positioned to determine what consumers want and source from a global network of low cost suppliers—a task manufacturers and retailers could not accomplish on their own. Not only can functions be shifted to the most efficient institutions in a channel; in a consumer-driven economy, they *will* be, as surely as tomorrow's sunrise, whenever markets are free enough to allow it.

Traditional supply chains begin with the producers of goods and services—their resources, goals, and market understanding. This model is really backwards. For example, there is no crude oil in the ground looking to turn jet turbines and automobile transmissions but, rather, people looking to get from Point A to Point B. Consumer markets start with the mind of consumers and then work *backwards* through the supply chain. This new way of viewing markets is described in Dr. Blackwell's book *From Mind to Market* (HarperBusiness, 1997) as a *demand chain*, "a non-linear, boundary-spanning process" depicted in Exhibits 4.3 and 4.4. At firms such as Amazon.com, Cisco Systems and Best Buy, the process is sometimes described as *customer-centricity.*

In third-party payer health care systems, the roles of producers (hospitals, physicians, manufacturers) are rigidly defined and consumers (patients) are the recipients of what producers plan and deliver. In consumer driven health care, the roles and responsibilities of health care providers begin by understanding the lifestyles and behavior of consumers. The firms best able to perform marketing functions do so, meaning products don't necessarily originate from manufacturers or providers (hospitals, physicians, etc.) but are developed at any point and by any player in the chain.

The best demand chain players use knowledge and innovative capability rather than size or position to gain a competitive edge. As described in *From Mind to Market*, organizations jockeying for the position of demand chain leader must be able to:

- Assimilate knowledge about consumers and the market
- Communicate that knowledge with other demand chain members and facilitate its implementation
- Adopt and promote a marketing orientation (customer-centricity) throughout the organization and demand chain
- Organize goals for the demand chain

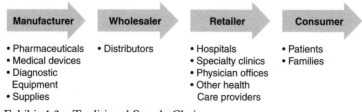

Exhibit 4.3   Traditional Supply Chain

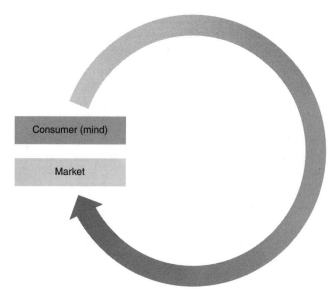

Exhibit 4.4   Demand Chain
Source: Roger Blackwell, *From Mind to Market* (HarperBusiness, 1997)

So, why haven't full-fledged demand chains appeared yet in health care delivery? The answer is simple, yet profound: consumers are not directly involved in paying the bills for routine, everyday health care costs.

Consumer Pain Cures Health Care's Woes

Consumers are beginning to get the message that just because they don't write the checks in the third-party payer system of the past, doesn't mean they don't pay the bills. Consumers feel the pain in their paychecks when their employer deducts a rising share of health insurance premiums. They feel it in higher co-pays when they visit the doctor or purchase a prescription, and they feel it in the bankrupting effects of uncovered catastrophic care. They even feel it when the 2.9 percent Medicare tax is deducted from their paychecks. As a consumer, would you rather your valuable health care dollars go to accountants or physicians, to paperwork or pharmaceuticals?

When the pain of high health care costs becomes unbearable, consumers will assert themselves, rebel against high prices and long waits, and force the health care supply chain to become more efficient. Health care companies will then have to do what visionary companies in other industries have done—take command of the supply chain and change it into a demand chain. Tapping the minds of health care consumers, understanding their expectations and preferences, how they will pay, and how their lifestyles affect the level of care needed represents the first step.

Demand chain leaders will need to use knowledge of consumer behavior to develop services and products people will buy at prices they are willing to pay. They will combine and outsource billing, streamline the way they buy medical supplies, develop specialized diagnostic facilities, hire specialists from regional medical organizations, adopt standardized reporting codes, and employ many other methods that shift essential marketing functions to the most efficient institutions in the demand chain. When that happens, smart, young, healthy consumers will be able to pay $800 a year for their health insurance and put several thousand dollars into a Health Savings Account which, if they remain healthy, can accumulate to pay much of their health care in later years. You can bet they will reward innovative firms that achieve competitive superiority in such attributes as price, efficiency, speed to market, and accuracy and point those that don't change in the direction of failure.

Health care institutions that benchmark themselves against the stellar, visionary firms of other industries not only have a bright future, they will reduce health care costs to a percentage of GDP that restores the United States to a more competitive place in the global economy and makes jobs more secure.

Case Study: Intermountain Health Care

Intermountain Health Care (IHC), based in Salt Lake City, Utah, is a health care provider that has leveraged organizational synergies, information technology, and economies of scale to reduce indirect health care costs.

Originally a loose affiliation of 15 hospitals owned by the Church of Jesus Christ of Latter-day Saints (LDS or Mormon), IHC now has 22 hospitals, 400 employed physicians, 2,300 affiliated physicians, and health plans in Utah, southern Idaho and southwestern Wyoming. It is estimated that 50 percent of hospital admissions and 40 to 60 percent of Utah's total health care expenditures are controlled by IHC. Despite its monopoly power, IHC charges patients 27 percent less than the national average and 15 percent less than non-IHC hospitals in Utah and pays market rates to participating physicians. Since 1975 when the LDS Church "donated" its 15 hospitals to this independent, secular, nonprofit organization, IHC has never experienced a year in the red. A model of efficiency, IHC consistently earns national recognition in the Top 100 Hospitals, Top 10 Heart Transplant Programs, Health Care's Most Wired, and the Top 100 Integrated Networks.

Key to IHC's success are highly integrated systems and operations, clear communication of system-wide goals, continuous performance improvement and focused growth. IHC's early leadership saw advantages of a statewide health care delivery system including economies of scale in purchasing and administrative functions, the ability to recruit top management, and improved quality through shared specialization. True to its Mormon roots of thrift and prudence, IHC's mission remains to "provide the best quality care at the lowest possible cost." Each hospital has a local board consisting of unpaid community members who promote charitable care, education, and lower health care costs.

Last, IHC felt that by owning its own health plans, it would attain cost savings and improve quality of care through shared information. Up-to-the-minute medical records on any IHC health plan member can be obtained instantly at any IHC facility, regardless of whether it is the flagship LDS Hospital in Salt Lake City or a rural family practice office in Idaho. This allows IHC to better manage the "longitudinal care of the patient, providing an understanding and accountability for the patient's health outside the hospital setting."

The Medical Malpractice Problem

Once consumers take control of their health care expenditures, not only will they attack inefficiency in the delivery of health care by utilizing the most effective and efficient providers, they will become informed about other nonvalue added health care costs.

Every time consumers check out of a hospital or a physician's office, a substantial part of their bill is to pay for malpractice insurance. Check the financial statements of your hospital, and you will find the

Table 4.5: Success Factors at Intermountain Health Care

Intermountain Health Care places a strong emphasis on setting and achieving goals. So much so that 20 percent of executives' salaries are tied directly to their accomplishments. IHC's Health Plan Division provides a good example of the types of goals set for the various business operations. The division's CEO, Sid Paulsen, outlines its goals for 2002:

Reducing medical expense. "Of a $1 premium, 89.5 cents goes to pay medical expense, meaning hospital, physician, lab, X-ray, pharmacy and so forth. One of our goals is to achieve a 10 percent or less trend rate."

Improving provider relations. "We do that with satisfaction scores. For example, 'Improve the satisfaction with health plans' policies and procedures between Q1 and Q4 surveys.' We send out a satisfaction survey every quarter to key physicians and office managers. We want to know that the things we're doing are making a difference."

Improving customer satisfaction service scores. "These are outlined in a couple of areas. For example, 'Implement at least one significant recommendation coming from the employer council by end of the fourth quarter.' In our regions, we put together councils of employers, some of our major and smaller customers, and they give us a barometer of how we're doing. We'll take an area where we're not doing as well-let's say on a five-point scale, we're at a 3.8, whereas for others we're at 4.4. We'll take the 3.8 and say we want to make a measurable difference. It can't be 3.85. It can be 3.9 or 3.91 or better, but it has to be measurable."

Growing IHC membership. "We need to grow at least at the same rate as the population in the state of Utah. We have 20 percent or 22 percent market share of the state's population. If the population grows by 50,000 people, we need approximately 20 percent of that 50,000 group to maintain our efficiency. That's net growth, so if 20,000 members drop out, we need to get 30,000 new members to maintain a net gain of 10,000."

Successfully implementing a new claims system. "We're in the process of implementing a claims system that would allow us to process a greater number of our claims electronically. That's a significant financial obligation, and we need to be on target and on budget."

Improving employee or team effectiveness. "IHC sends out a survey to the employees each year in September with various questions focusing on how do employees rate their managers, whether strategies and values of the company are clear, and so forth. We choose one of those areas to improve. This year we picked the area of communication between one-year-or-less employees and supervisory people."

SOURCE: Intermountain Health Care Health Plan Division CEO Sid Paulson

hospital is paying more, often much more, for malpractice insurance than all of its utilities—electricity, gas, and water—combined. Skyrocketing malpractice insurance premiums are driving specialists out of some high-risk specialties, forcing part-time or semi-retired physicians completely out of practice, and leaving some communities completely without critical specialties. New standards of practice have risen, not based on medical need or efficiency, but from the pervasive fear of litigation. In some cases, the ability of physicians and patients to talk openly is no longer permitted by lawyers who advise physicians to avoid communicating with patients.

Although some consumers perceive malpractice to be as loosely defined as a physician's inability to bring about a cure for the patient, in actuality it is defined as "dereliction from professional duty or a failure to exercise an accepted degree of professional skill or learning by a person (such as a physician) rendering professional services, which results in injury, loss or damage." From the consumer perspective, malpractice is a two-dimensional problem.

First is the occurrence of actual malpractice and its detrimental effect on a patient's health. Second is the increased cost of health care attributed to alleged or real malpractice. About half of malpractice suits are regarded as "nuisance" suits where there is no finding of fault and no award (although legal fees are still incurred). The actual costs to the health care system are much greater because of costs associated with "defensive medicine"—tests and procedures based on the threat of litigation rather than medical need. A study of Texas physicians found that the wave of malpractice claims resulted in the following practices by doctors:

- 67 percent were ordering more x-rays
- 66 percent were ordering more lab test
- 51 percent made greater use of a second physician's opinion
- 50 percent were delegating less responsibility for the patient's care to other medical personnel
- 48 percent were hospitalizing their patients more often

The severity of the malpractice problem is summarized in testimony before the National Conference on Medical Malpractice held by the Subcommittee on Health and the Environment of the U.S. House of Representatives. The problems are described in the box on the opposite page.

How Does Malpractice Affect Health Care?

Physicians face these major problems:

1. The skyrocketing costs of malpractice insurance is forcing some physicians to retire early, and new, young physicians to enter other areas rather than open up practice
2. The system by which malpractice claims are settled is extremely costly to them and subsequently to their patients as rates continue to escalate
3. They are forced to practice defensive medicine
4. They fear that in a profession that depends upon the trust and confidence of their patients, medical malpractice is contributing to erosion of the relationship
5. The contingent fee system of paying lawyers is an incentive for them to aim for a high settlement from the physician

Hospitals face these problems:

1. Hospitals are being severely criticized for their escalating costs, and yet the increases in their medical malpractice insurance are forcing these costs up further
2. The present approach reduces quality of care
3. The practice of defensive medicine on the part of their physicians forces hospitals to hire more people, purchase more equipment and material, and thereby increases their costs

Lawyers face these problems:

1. The contingent fee system is being seriously questioned and yet it allows for the poor as well as the rich to be equally represented
2. They are accused of being overly aggressive and suit-oriented where medical malpractice claims are concerned
3. Medical malpractice claims require more of their time than other personal injury claims
4. Docket delays are significant as is case duration

Insurers face these problems:

1. The inability to predict with reasonable accuracy the number and size of claims that might arise from providers' encounters with patients
2. The relative small number of insurance providers and the harmful impact a single very large award can have on reserves and rates
3. Inflation and its impact on future settlements
4. The concern that courts are increasingly making awards in the case of injuries whether or not negligence has been proven

What Are the Possible Solutions?

The following alternatives could dramatically reduce the costs of malpractice and still maintain equity among patient and provider interests:

1. Arbitration, in which patients and providers agree to let a state or federal organization appoint skilled arbitrators to settle malpractice claims. The agreement could be a condition for purchasing health care from most providers, much as it is for purchasing investments from a brokerage firm or finance professional.

2. Government malpractice insurance, in which a state or federal agency, similar to workers' compensation, collects malpractice insurance premiums from all physicians and decides what benefits would be given to all patients with malpractice claims.

3. State or federal laws which restrict the amounts that can be collected by patients for malpractice claims, usually actual costs plus a limited amount (such as $250,000) for punitive damages.

4. Peer group certification, in which a group of physicians and other professionals (including a consumer ombudsperson) review malpractice claims and decide which ones can be taken to trial.

5. Contingency fee limits, in which legislation limits the proportion of the settlement that lawyers can receive for malpractice suits.

6. Contractual release, signed by persons receiving health care services agreeing not to sue for malpractice, in return for lower health care fees and free care when mistakes occur.

7. Communication time, in which physicians provide additional oral and written communications about the risks of providing health care (although this might incur higher initial fees).

8. Mandated risk assignment, in which federal or state governments require insurance companies to reduce malpractice rates to doctors in return for corresponding higher rates on health insurance to the general public.

9. Counter suits by physicians against patients and their attorneys who sue for malpractice without adequate basis for the malpractice suit.

There is widespread support for several of these approaches, especially those that limit contingency fees and awards for punitive damages. Malpractice litigation may occur in situations where malpractice actually occurs or in situations where no malpractice occurs. Arbitration works in many areas of business and there is substantial support for arbitration as a way of lowering total costs to the health care system and yet providing relief in those cases in which malpractice does occur. Arbitration would require the creation of a new administrative body, but it solves the most important problem in underwriting malpractice insurance—large, unpredictable awards that are very difficult to handle as actuarial risks. It also eliminates a portion of attorney costs although some provision is needed to represent consumers unable to pay or unfamiliar with the legal process. The most immediately feasible alternative is a federal law that places reasonable limits on punitive awards. Combined with high deductible policies, that would reduce dramatically the cost of malpractice insurance and promote a normal allocation of physicians by specialty and geographic location.

Malpractice lawyers who benefit greatly from the current system can be expected to oppose changes, but if you are concerned about the cost of malpractice insurance as a consumer, and if you want a physician available in your area to treat you (especially if you want one who delivers babies), you must enlist in the battle against escalating malpractice insurance costs.

Health Care Fraud

Fraud adds about $500 per year to individual health insurance premiums. According to most estimates, it now accounts for seven to 10 percent of total health care expenditures, or more than $150 billion annually, although some researchers believe the amount is as high as 30 percent. With regard to Medicare and Medicaid, consumers pay for fraud through increased taxes, fewer benefits, fewer people covered, and funds diverted from other government programs. In privately insured health care, consumers pay through higher premiums, higher co-pays, higher deductibles, lower wages, and in the long run, fewer jobs for America's citizens. As a consumer in consumer driven health care, you have many reasons to support antifraud programs, including its risks for patients. Fraud taints permanent medical records, exhausts lifetime medical benefits, and creates risk of physical injury or death. From an economic perspective, health care fraud creates competitive disadvantage for legitimate, high quality providers, corrupting the health care system for all consumers.

What is health care fraud? Fraud includes *any intentional or deliberate act to deprive another of money or property by guile, deception, or other unfair means.* Four elements are present in fraud, regardless of whether the act is criminal or civil: a materially false statement, knowledge of its falsity, reliance on the false statement by the victim, and damages suffered as a result of reliance. HIPAA specifically establishes health care fraud as a federal criminal offense (US Code, Title 17, Section 1347), punishable by a prison term of up to 10 years in addition to significant financial penalties. Fraud that results in injury of a patient may double the prison term up to 20 years, while fraud that results in death may result in life imprisonment.

In today's third-party payer system, most fraud is defined as either provider or recipient fraud, both of which involve defrauding the third-party payer. Examples are shown in the box on the opposite page. Additional forms of fraud preying on consumers, including corporate abuse and scams, are addressed later in the chapter.

Examples of Fraud in Third-Party Payer Systems

Provider Fraud

1. Billing for services not provided
   - Charges for nonexistent patients
   - Padding claims with fictitious procedures
2. Misrepresentation of services
   - Billing uncovered services as covered services (miscoding)
3. Misrepresentation of dates of service
   - Billing for services rendered to a patient during a period they were not insured
4. Misrepresentation of a patient's condition
   - Billing for more complex procedures than are medically necessary to receive higher reimbursement ("up coding")
5. Misrepresentation of the charge for a service
   - Failure to report discounts given to the patient
   - Altering the charge on a claim to more than what was actually charged
   - Billing separately for individual services supposed to be reimbursed together at a lower rate (unbundling)

6. Misrepresentation of identity
   • Billing services administered to an uninsured patient under another person's policy
7. Paying kickbacks for patient referrals
   • Incentives paid for patients to feign symptoms and accept care for medically unnecessary procedures
   • Offer of "free" medical services, luring patients to provide confidential insurance information for use in fraudulent billings

Provider Fraud

1. Applications for coverage
   • Omitting or misrepresenting information (including previous medical treatment) on an application for benefits
   • Obtaining coverage for nonemployees by representing them as members of a covered group
   • Underreporting income to become Medicaid-eligible
   • Hiding assets to obtain nursing home coverage
   • Misrepresenting household composition
   • Misrepresenting residency to obtain or maintain Medicare or Medicaid coverage in another state
2. Accident reports
   • Providing false information to receive benefits under an insurance contract's accident benefit
3. Coordination of benefits
   • Withholding information about other insurance coverage to obtain duplicate reimbursements

Provider and recipient fraud is significant in the nearly $600 billion spent in 2004 on Medicare and Medicaid. Current public assistance programs are slow to modernize technology and use outdated claims processing systems (many of which are paper-based) where volume often exceeds capacity. A "pay and chase" mentality emphasizes quick payment of claims over validity and the need to retain providers willing to accept Medicaid reimbursement (notoriously below market) results in provider lists that are almost never purged, with up to 50 percent of listed providers "inactive." Added to complicated reimbursement procedures that require extensive coding, there is ample opportunity for fraud. The good news, however, is that the problem is fixable.

The most effective antifraud programs are those that create sufficient controls to limit opportunities for fraud. *Compliance* strategies provide economic incentives for voluntary compliance to the laws plus use of administrative efforts to control violations before they occur, achieving the long-term objective of influencing *behavior*. When people believe fraud is likely to be detected, they are more likely to comply with the rules. *Deterrence* occurs by detecting law violations, determining who is responsible, and penalizing offenders. Effectiveness is achieved by controlling immediate behavior of violators and instilling belief among potential violators they would also be detected and punished.

The key to stopping health care fraud is better data systems, focusing on data matching and data mining. In *data mining*, processes match multiple databases to identify exceptions and violations, much the way the Internal Revenue Services matches computer generated payments by employers and financial institutions to computer analyzed returns of taxpayers. Data mining involves thorough analysis of databases to identify patterns and anomalies. With data mining, payments are analyzed to identify outliers, unusual growth rates, impossible combinations of services, and to conduct peer comparisons. The box on the that follows summarizes steps that can be taken to stop health care fraud.

Steps to Stop Health Care Fraud

1. Make fighting fraud an organizational priority.
2. Train staff at all levels to identify fraudulent activity.
3. Focus on highest risk services and provider types first.
4. Use an array of analysis tools to test for fraud throughout the reimbursement process. (Prepayment edits catch fraud before a payment is made.)
5. Use the past to predict the future. Generally detection of one fraud indicates extensive fraud or control weaknesses to specific services, providers, patients, etc.
6. Analyze ways controls may be avoided or compromised.
7. Pursue investigations through prosecution or until all funds have been recovered.
8. Reinvest recovered funds in fraud prevention efforts.

Provider and recipient fraud are natural consequences of a health care system controlled by distant third-party payers. Once consumers take control of their own health care spending through Health Savings Accounts, much of the indirect health care costs of provider and recipient fraud will be eliminated. However, just because the battle is won doesn't mean the war is over. In an open consumer market for health care services, consumers will still have to be aware of the potential for corporate abuse and scams.

Corporate Fraud and Abuse

In spite of laws attacking health care fraud, corporate examples abound that illustrate the potential for breaking laws. Consider the alleged misdeeds of HealthSouth Corporation. Founded in 1984 by CEO Richard Scrushy (then a 29-year-old respiratory therapist) with $50,000 cash, the company went public in 1986. By 2003, Health-South was the largest provider of outpatient surgery, diagnostic and rehabilitative health care services in the United States and operated 1,800 inpatient and outpatient rehabilitation facilities, outpatient surgery centers, diagnostic centers, medical centers and other health care facilities worldwide.

Two trends fueled the company's growth. First, changes in Medicare laws rewarded higher margins to health care providers who could manage their costs. Second, a baby boomer population that worshipped exercise was hitting middle age and beginning to suffer from wear and tear. The latter played well to Scrushy's vision of removing physical therapy from the dark corners of hospitals, transformed into star status at his "Hospital of the Future." Scrushy used sports stars such as Alabama native Bo Jackson and a rock-and-roll band sponsored by HealthSouth Entertainment, to promote the hospital's rehabilitation programs. But earnings grew less rapidly than aspirations, resulting in charges that HealthSouth overstated earnings by $1.4 billion over five years. Reported earnings exceeded actual earnings by 4,700 percent between 1999 and 2002. Inflated earnings were balanced by overstating assets, which by 2002 exceeded $800 million or 10 percent of total assets.

A forensic audit in 2004 by PriceWaterhouseCoopers reported $3.9 to $4.6 billion in accounting irregularities from 1996 through 2002. If the results didn't meet expectations, the CEO allegedly ordered the CFO to record false accounting entries to cover the shortfall. CEO Scrushy and other HealthSouth executives reaped massive profits from stock options and salary and bonus based on stock performance. Among other "perks," HealthSouth maintained for its senior officers as many as 12 airplanes, a helicopter, and a 92–foot yacht. The result of these activities was an 85–count fraud indictment, carrying a maximum penalty of 650 years in prison and $36 million in fines, along with forfeiture of $278 million in property.

Scams

Consumer health care scams run the gamut from fake insurance to bogus Medicare drug cards. Some give the appearance of "full coverage," for as low as $89/month with no questions asked, but in reality only provide "discounts" at a limited or nonexistent network of providers. Even if legitimate coverage is provided, there may be strict limitations written into the fine print. In one instance, a patient was stuck with more than $500,000 in charges for cancer treatment because the fine print in his insurance policy capped chemotherapy treatment at $1,000 per day when in reality it cost $18,000. In another instance, a scam operator sold full health insurance to pregnant women at a cost of $3,000, but altered their applications to make it appear as though they were employees of a third-party corporation. After pocketing the $2,000 difference between his fee and the cost of group coverage, the insurance company uncovered the scam and denied $2.3 million in claims by the fake employees, sending their bills to collections agencies. The General Accounting Office has found that 144 unlicensed health insurers covering 200,000 people have left $252 million in unpaid medical claims in recent years.

With the number of uninsured Americans at 45 million, and small business constituting the fastest growing segment of the economy, conditions are ripe for more health care scams. Between 2000 and 2004, the number of individuals buying their own health insurance jumped 1.5 million to 17.5 million, meaning there are literally thousands of people out there looking for a bargain. This number is likely to increase with the proliferation of Health Savings Accounts, putting more responsibility for good information in the hands of consumers in consumer driven health care. Ideally, regulatory bodies should provide information on the viability of different health plans, as the FDIC now does with financial institutions. For now, however, the onus is on consumers to research and do business only with reputable firms.

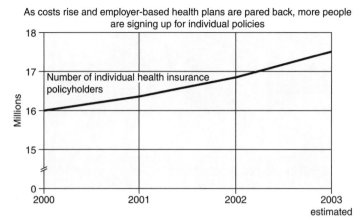

As costs rise and employer-based health plans are pared back, more people are signing up for individual policies

Exhibit 4.6   Source: BusinessWeek, July 5, 2004

Winning the War

There are many battles in the war on health care costs, but none has as big an impact as the one against indirect costs. If we could eliminate all indirect costs, it would solve more than half of America's "Two Trillion Dollar Crisis." The first step is to move from an inherently inefficient system of third-party payers to consumer driven health care. Once that is accomplished, consumers will drive expenditures to the most efficient and effective providers, improving quality and lowering total costs.

CHAPTER 5

The Crisis of the Direct Costs of Health Care

"I don't know who discovered water, but it probably wasn't a fish."
—Marshall McCluan

Sixty percent of the nearly two trillion dollars America spends on health care is not for *care* at all, as you saw in Chapter 4, but rather massive amounts of overhead that add little to consumer health and wellness. Although it's logical to attack these indirect costs first, we must not neglect the remaining 40 percent—the direct costs of health care including the services of physicians, nurses and other health care providers. Unfortunately, the people who own, staff and manage health care institutions are like fish swimming in the river of health care costs. So long as third-party payers set the rules and write the checks, health care practitioners are held captive. But when consumers take control, considerable change will occur.

Too Much Demand and Too Little Supply

Hospital care and clinical services make up more than 50 percent of the direct costs of health care, as shown in Exhibit 5.1. As every student of economics learns, nothing affects price so much as the interaction of supply and demand. With advances in medical technology turning once fatal illnesses into long-term managed conditions, and massive numbers of baby boomers headed toward the years of most intensive health care needs, there is no question demand is increasing. The question that has to be answered is, "Will there be enough physicians and nurses to provide the care they need?" The answer leads to the troubling diagnosis of too much demand and too little supply of qualified health care providers, leading to less care at higher prices.

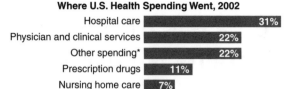

Where U.S. Health Spending Went, 2002

Hospital care	31%
Physician and clinical services	22%
Other spending*	22%
Prescription drugs	11%
Nursing home care	7%
Program administration	7%

*Includes dentist services, home health care, durable medical products, over-the-counter medicines, public health, research and construction

Exhibit 5.1

Who Will Take Care of Us?
Part I: Nurses and Medical Technicians

Hospital administrators recognize that about 45 to 60 percent of a typical hospital's budget is devoted to labor and there are really only two possible solutions to reduce or limit increases in the cost of skilled labor:

1. Increase the supply of skilled hospital labor, or
2. Increase the productivity of existing personnel.

If you've been to a hospital recently, you've probably already observed a critical shortage of health care professionals needed to provide quality care. To fill the gap, many hospitals are left no choice but to "import" physicians, nurses, x-ray and laboratory technicians, physical and occupational therapists and other ancillary staff from other nations like the Philippines, South Africa, and India, helping workers overcome immigration barriers to relocate in the United States. Not only does this practice drain vital resources from sometimes poorer countries, but language and cultural barriers often impair communication, a critical skill in patient care.

Without additional personnel, existing professionals must become more productive by working longer hours and spending less time per patient—both of which lead to lower job satisfaction and a reduced quality of patient care. Working long, grueling hours including nights, weekends, and holidays with little time off leads to burn out, accelerating the rate at which qualified personnel leave patient care for other job opportunities.

Efforts to unionize are gaining momentum with the Service Employees International Union (SEIU) recruiting hospital personnel throughout the nation. At Northern Michigan Hospital in Petoskey, Michigan, a nursing strike declared in 2002 lasted more than two years after nurses selected the International Brotherhood of Teamsters as their representative. The efforts of nurses' unions to reduce workloads and increase staffing levels have led to such shortages in California that some hospitals have closed. Where hospitals have been unable to recruit sufficient new numbers of nurses, the take-home pay of existing nurses has risen to that of some physicians. Although prior attempts for physicians to merge practice groups to provide greater negotiating power with third-party payers have been challenged as antitrust, what would happen to health care prices if physicians were likewise able to unionize?

The shortage of qualified medical personnel can be dangerous to patient health. What happens when a patient with internal bleeding lies for hours in an emergency room waiting for a blood transfusion because nobody is available to transport him to the machine located on another floor of the hospital? Or when an elderly patient needing assistance to the bathroom waits 45 minutes after pushing her call button for someone to arrive?

The most pressing shortage of workers is in nursing, which is blamed for 31 percent more postsurgery deaths in hospitals unable to cope with the nursing shortage (*New York Times,* "The Last Shift," March 16, 2003). When the State of California passed legislation requiring hospitals to have qualified, surplus nursing staff standing by to provide fill-in coverage anytime an assigned nurse leaves his or her post, the Santa Teresita Hospital in Duarte, California closed its doors because it could not come up with enough nurses to staff the hospital. As of publication, the debate over nursing ratios has taken center stage in California, with some arguing one nurse to every five patients is appropriate and others claiming one to six is sufficient. If nurse-to-patient ratios are set at a level that hospitals cannot maintain compliance, nursing salaries will skyrocket, immigration will accelerate (perhaps taking nurses from other areas of desperate need unable to pay such high salaries), and, like Santa Teresita, some hospitals will close. If you're planning surgery in the next fifteen years, keep in mind that the Bureau of Health Statistics concludes that we will have a shortage of 800,000 nurses by the year 2020, as shown in Exhibit 5.2.

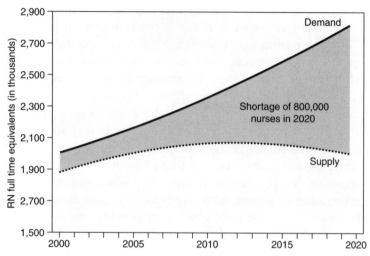

Exhibit 5.2   Supply vs. Demand for Registered Nurses, 2000–2020
Source: Project Supply, Demand and Shortages of Registered Nurses,
2000–2020. Bureau of Health.

The Nursing Shortage

There are about 2.7 million licensed nurses in the United States, but 500,000 of them are not working in patient care, choosing alternative careers such as practice management, insurance review, medical research, and pharmaceutical sales (Berlinger and Ginsberg, "Why This Hospital Nursing Shortage is Different," 2000). Women whose career options may have once been limited to traditionally female-dominated careers such as nursing and teaching have made great progress in penetrating medicine, law, business, and engineering in equal numbers. However, despite the potential for high pay and steady employment, few men are pursuing nursing. Some institutions have attempted to overcome stereotypes and recruit more men to their nursing schools. The University of North Carolina at Chapel Hill, features males equally in its marketing materials and provides an innovative summer camp for high school boys with hands-on experience in patient care. Despite these efforts, male enrollment in UNC's baccalaureate nursing programs is still less than eight percent—similar to other schools in its region. By contrast, at UNC's School of Medicine, 51 percent of the 663 students pursing the M.D. degree in 2004 are female. Nationally, women submitted 37 percent of all medical school applications in 1986, 42 percent in 1996 and more than 50 percent in 2004.

Of course, there is also the logic that if a student is going to work so hard as to become a nurse, why not just become a doctor? Despite the greater numbers of nurses required for patient care, at the University of Mississippi Medical Center in Jackson, there were 438 medical students but only 211 nursing students in 2003, and between 1998 and 2003, nursing school enrollment fell by 45 percent while medical school enrollment remained flat. Leading universities nationwide report similar statistics.

Nursing school enrollment hit all-time lows in the 1980s and 90s resulting in a nursing work force that currently averages 45 years of age, with only 9.1 percent of nurses younger than 30. Who will take care of the baby boomers at a time when many of the baby boomer nurses will become patients themselves? Some have proposed replacing nurses altogether with technicians who can perform many of the same tasks. As medicine becomes more complex, well-trained and highly-skilled people are needed for the job whether they are nurses, physicians' assistants or other medical technicians.

Working conditions are part of the problem and in some hospitals nursing staffs turn over as frequently as every 18 months. Many young nurses balancing the obligations of career and family want time to care for their children. Innovative hospitals are experimenting with flexible working schedules, in many cases shifting from five eight-hour days to three twelve-hour days. But such is difficult to accomplish if there are insufficient personnel to cover undesirable night and weekend shifts. Some hospitals have added on-premise childcare while others simply resort to overtime for the few nurses willing to accept long shifts (sometimes in return for high wages) or pools of "traveling nurses" who fill in, at about three times the normal wage rate, when a hospital is so short of nurses that it faces impaired patient care. The result is not only high labor costs for the hospital, but sometimes dangerous situations in which nurses trained for one specialty or knowledgeable with the systems of different institutions are thrown into unfamiliar tasks or situations simply because there is no one else available.

As you read in Chapter 2, men and women once employed in jobs that have been eliminated by globalization have not been fully integrated into the nursing profession, leaving hospital administrators little choice but to raise salaries and pursue foreign-trained nurses.

Despite increased demand, nursing school capacity has remained flat, and shortages in state and federal funds have resulted in the number of qualified nursing applicants exceeding several times the number of classroom openings. Training programs in nursing are often understaffed, underfunded and ineffective in attracting the young men and women so desperately needed in nursing and other skilled health care jobs. In addition, hospital-based and two-year technical programs that once provided the bulk of the nursing workforce have been replaced by baccalaureate programs producing more educated and better-trained nurses, but ones who also have work options other than patient care. Clearly, we have a supply problem.

The barriers to finding students to fill these needs are:

1. Too few faculty members to staff nursing schools
2. Too few classrooms
3. Too few clinical sites to handle qualified applicants
4. Little funding and high costs for students

Direct patient care is facing a crisis if health care institutions do not develop a coordinated, integrated effort to attract qualified applicants and increase the number of nursing and technical programs. The best solution is to offer flex-time, part-time, and other flexible scheduling arrangements to accommodate parents desiring to adapt their schedules to meet the needs of their children, yet still function as skilled health care professionals. Such would provide for continuity of services to patients and institutions. In addition to the job retraining programs proposed in Chapter 2, national priorities should consider forgiving the debt of students who graduate from qualified programs after they complete a period of time (maybe five years) in direct patient care.

When third-party payers no longer constrain what health care providers can do, who must do which jobs and how much they can get paid for it, an open market for health care services develops with consumers migrating to the health care providers that meet their needs most efficiently and effectively. In consumer driven health care, health care institutions must change their expectations and improve working conditions in order to recruit qualified individuals for patient care. That involves working with colleges and universities and the government to bring about more favorable policies increasing accessibility and enrollment in existing programs or developing new and innovative programs for nontraditional personnel.

> *Solution to America's "Two Trillion Dollar Crisis": Establish national and/or state programs to attract qualified applicants to nursing and health care technician programs that include funding a program to forgive nurses their nursing school education debt after five years of hospital experience.*

Who Will Take Care of Us?
Part II: Physicians

Unless America acts, it will also face a physician shortage in the next 25 years. The U.S. population is expected to grow to 309 million by 2010, 336 million by 2020, and 420 million by 2050 based upon projections of births, deaths, and net immigration. Yet, current medical school enrollment remains flat, creating a "sellers market" for medical school graduates that further increases the direct costs of health care.

If the current ratio of physicians to the total population is applied to anticipated growth and the number of physicians expected to be practicing is calculated by projecting medical school graduation rates and subtracting the number of physicians expected to retire, in approximately 25 years the United States will face a shortage of 300,000 physicians, soaring to 500,000 by 2050 as shown in Exhibit 5.3. If these numbers are not scary enough, consider the following additional factors.

First, these numbers assume that the ratio of physicians to population will stay at its current level. Between 1960 and 2000, the ratio

Exhibit 5.3   Physician Needs and Shortages

Decade	Population	Physicians Needed	Physicians Practicing	Shortage
2010	309,000,000	883,740	787,600	96,140
2020	336,000,000	960,960	757,400	203,560
2030	364,000,000	1,041,040	727,200	313,840
2040	392,000,000	1,121,120	697,000	424,120
2050	420,000,000	1,201,200	697,000	504,200

increased substantially from 140 to 286 physicians per 100,000 population. Medical science has allowed patients with chronic long-term illnesses to live longer, but more physicians are required for their care. As baby boomers age and demand the most advanced medical treatment, especially for long-term illness, even more physicians will be required to meet their needs.

Second, the projected shortages do not account for the obesity epidemic. Some experts believe that, if current trends continue, by 2030 nearly 100 percent of Americans will be obese. Obesity associates with diabetes, heart disease, cancer, and a host of other ailments requiring significant lifetime medical care. Unless America starts winning the war on obesity, described in Chapter 9, the physician shortage will be even greater than projected.

Third, new residency rules formulated by the American Association for Graduate Medical Education stating that a resident can work only 80 hours per week averaged over a month and must get one day off every week reduce available working hours for the nation's approximately 112,000 medical residents and fellows by 20 percent, equivalent to the loss of 22,000 full-time positions.

Fourth, projected physician shortages are based on past practices, assuming a forty-year career before retirement after graduation from medical school at age 25 or 26. The average retirement age of surgeons is now 58, down from 71 a decade ago, although physicians in some specialties like internal medicine typically practice longer than surgeons. Physicians blame frustrations with managed care, bureaucratic red tape, loss of autonomy, diminished prestige, and deep personal dissatisfaction. Not only have Medicaid, Medicare, and private insurance reimbursement fallen by almost 60 percent since 1991, but when high overhead, uncollectible receivables and skyrocketing malpractice insurance premiums prevent physicians from making a profit after all expenses are paid, many simply retire at a time they might otherwise only reduce their workloads. The malpractice insurance problem described in Chapter 4 is particularly troubling. In Ohio, the nation's "bellweather" state, premiums at the top five malpractice insurance underwriters have increased an average of 31 percent annually over the past three years. Today, most surgeons in Ohio pay an average $110,000 annually for malpractice insurance. If the malpractice reforms described in Chapter 4 are not adopted, expect early retirement to contribute to even greater physician shortages.

Solving the Physician Shortage Crisis

How can the United States solve its physician shortage? One solution is to import the half million additional physicians needed by 2050 from other nations. Most hospitals will extend admitting privileges to qualified foreign medical graduates who have completed their residency at a U.S. hospital. The percentage of international medical school graduates entering U.S. cardiology fellowships has increased progressively from 15 percent in 1970 to 39 percent in 2001 (Richard P. Lewis, M.D., "Crunch Time for Clinical Cardiology"). Currently foreign graduates make up 25 percent of all medical residents with the resulting trend toward more foreign trained residents, shown in Exhibit 5.4. If the physician shortage is not addressed, by 2050 American medical graduates will represent only 58 percent of the U.S. physician work force. Although immigration is a solution, is it such a good idea to rob 100,000 medical graduates each decade until 2050 from other, often seriously underserved nations while denying our own children the opportunity to advance into the medical profession? And what happens if the United States can no longer depend upon a steady stream of well-educated immigrants?

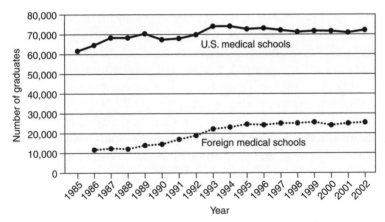

Exhibit 5.4   Graduates of Foreign and U.S. Medical Schools in Residency Programs in the United States, 1985 through 2002.
Graduates of Canadian medical schools and graduates of osteopathic schools are included in the numbers for U.S. medical schools. Data are from the Medical Education Theme Issues of the *Journal of the American Medical Association* from 1986 through 2003.

The economic miracle occurring in rapidly expanding markets like India and China has created new jobs for U.S. trained physicians and an incentive for them to return to their native countries. As democracy flourishes and standards of living rise around the globe, it could be more difficult for the United States to attract and retain physicians from other nations. One Iraqi physician recently spoke of his need 20 years ago to immigrate with his family to the United States to escape the persecution and hardship brought about by the regime of Saddam Hussein. Today that same physician wants to use his U.S. medical training and experience to shape the rebuilding of medical institutions in his homeland.

If we cannot import more foreign trained physicians, the alternative solution is to pay much higher salaries inducing physicians to work even longer hours. If we analyze the crisis at more fundamental levels, perhaps the better answer is found in recruiting more qualified applicants to medical schools and providing better resources for their training at a reasonable cost.

How Many Medical Students?

The United States is not producing a sufficient number of new doctors to carry the clinical load of its growing population. Between 1982 and 2002, the number of medical school applications dropped from 2.1 to 1.9 per seat. Although some observers believed the decline to be cyclical (as it appears on Exhibit 5.5 with medical school applications peaking in 1997 at 47,000 and then headed down again), what's significant is that this downward trend is continuing in spite of the 70–plus million members of Generation Y who are starting to graduate college and are ripe for graduate school. The problem is not a matter of preparation or intelligence, because undergraduate GPAs and MCAT scores are similar to previous classes. Rather, the culprit is student debt.

Decades ago, many medical students came from affluent families, able to finance the long, expensive education required to become a physician. Today, the profession has opened to the middle class resulting in average total educational debt of $103,000 in 2002, up from $80,462 in 1997, according to the Association of American Medical Colleges. The average total educational debt is expected to be around $130,000 for the class of 2006.

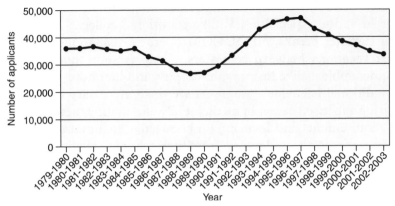

Exhibit 5.5   Applicants to U.S. Medical Schools, 1979 through 2003.
The numbers of applicants to U.S. medical schools have not shown a steady increase
or decrease during the past 20 years. Data are from the American Association of
Medical Colleges.

Although private foundations provide loans and scholarships to the most qualified applicants, it's probably time to consider additional alternatives in which highly-qualified medical students are supported directly during their education or have available programs which repay student debts as they complete specified periods of service, especially in areas of most critical need.

> *Solution to America's "Two Trillion Dollar Crisis": Congress and other institutions should evaluate current loan programs to consider alternative forms of debt forgiveness or direct subsidies to well-qualified medical students.*

Another alternative is to reduce the number of years of schooling required for physicians by combining undergraduate and graduate medical studies. At the Northeastern Ohio Universities College of Medicine (NEOUCOM) and 17 other accelerated programs around the nation, students apply to medical school in their senior year of high school. After completing premedical coursework for 12 to 15 months at partner institutions including the University of Akron, Kent State University, and Youngstown State University, students begin a rigorous 40–month program at NEOUCOM consisting of medical school, clerkships at affiliated teaching hospitals, and electives in various specialties. Unlike traditional colleges that provide long summer breaks, NEOUCOM operates year-round, providing short vacations between semesters. There is some question as to whether subjects like history, philosophy, and literature that are part of traditional bachelor's programs are really necessary for someone desiring a focused career in medicine. By eliminating these nonessential requirements and focusing on knowledge required to effectively practice medicine, students go from high school to residency in six or seven years as opposed to eight or nine years in traditional programs, paying less tuition and incurring less debt.

> *Solution to America's "Two Trillion Dollar Crisis": Expand the number of combined B.S./M.D. programs, eliminating unnecessary coursework and reducing the time and expense required to train physicians, putting more physicians into practice more quickly.*

In Search of Work/Life Balance

In today's hustle and bustle world that seems to leave little time for the most important things, employees across industries seek to have greater control over their work/life balance. It's one of the dominant themes found among the cohort of young people described by marketers as "GenerationY"—the "baby boom echo" currently in its teens and twenties. College students are increasingly abandoning undergraduate premedical studies, often citing disillusionment with the physician lifestyle.

Unlike the days of old, when physicians owned their own practices and thus set their own hours, hired their own staff, and built enduring relationships of loyalty and trust with patients, physicians today are employees of a third-party payer. As a result, many work "8 to 5" jobs, not much different from others in the corporate world. Studies of physicians' complaints include workload, administrative paperwork, limitations on referring patients to specialists of a physician's choosing, financial incentives to curb medical work-ups, and the physician's role as an agent for insurers, government agencies, and courts. Facing these issues, why would anyone expect physicians to put in longer hours than corporate lawyers, accountants or other well-educated professionals?

When the income, working hours, and years of required training for a medical career are considered, none approaches the explanatory power of controllable lifestyle. The specialty preferences of U.S. senior medical students reflect these lifestyle variables, particularly in internal medicine and general surgery. The number of medical students selecting internal medicine residencies declined from 26.6 percent to 24.8 percent between 1996 and 2002, according to the National Residency Matching Program. For general surgery, the decline was from 10.4 to 7.6 percent, representing 300 fewer general surgeons training each year and raising concerns about an adequate general surgery workforce. The concern is even greater for family practice, with residency programs declining from a 73 to 43 percent fill rate from 1996 to 2002.

Exhibit 5.6   Controllable lifestyle differences among selected specialties.

Specialty	Lifestyle	Average Income	Average Work Hours per Week	Years of Graduate Medical Education
Anesthesiology	Controllable	$225,000	61.0	4
Dermatology	Controllable	$221,000	45.5	4
Emergency Medicine	Controllable	$183,000	46.0	4
Family Practice	Uncontrollable	$132.000	52.5	3
Internal Medicine	Uncontrollable	$158,000	57.0	3
Neurology	Controllable	$172,000	55.5	4
Obstetrics/Gynecology	Uncontrollable	$224,000	61.0	4
Ophthalmology	Controllable	$225,000	47.0	4
Orthopedic Surgery	Uncontrollable	$323,000	58.0	5
Otolaryngology	Controllable	$242,000	53.5	5
Pathology	Controllable	$202,000	45.5	4
Pediatrics	Uncontrollable	$136,000	54.0	3
Psychiatry	Controllable	$134,000	48.0	4
Radiology	Controllable	$263,000	58.0	4
General Surgery	Uncontrollable	$238,000	60.0	5
Urology	Uncontrollable	$245,000	60.5	5
Average	**N/A**	**$208,000**	**53.9**	**4**

Despite these challenges, medicine is still a rewarding profession, both clinically and materially. Financially, the median salaries of representative specialties are represented in Exhibit 5.7 by the following data collected by the Medical Group Management Association, reported in 2003:

Exhibit 5.7

Specialty	Median Salary
Anesthesiologist	$281,963
Cardiologist	$320,111
Emergency Medicine	$170,329
Family Practice Without OB	$146,601
Internal Medicine	$149,220
Orthopedic Surgeon	$354,184
General Surgeon	$257,509
Cardiovascular Surgeon	$459,011

These are high incomes compared to the average worker in America, but the average worker also does not have a college degree requiring at least four years of highly competitive study, four years of rigorous medical school, a residency of three to seven years and accumulated debt exceeding $100,000. Add the problem of malpractice insurance premiums exceeding $100,000 a year in many specialties and the high numbers of uncollectible receivables and it's easy to see why consumers should be concerned about who, if anyone, will be there to take care of them in the future.

Alternatively Skilled Health Care Providers

In many cases, traditional health care providers, including medical doctors and registered nurses, are not the most effective or efficient providers of care. Nurse practitioners, physician assistants, emergency medical technicians and an array of other specialists are often more proficient in specific tasks than generalist physicians. For example, diabetics who are seen on a regular basis at a special outpatient clinic staffed by nurses may do better than similar patients seen as needed by a family physician. In Canada, Germany and other nations, midwives provide the majority of routine maternity care. Pharmacists are skilled at recommending over-the-counter remedies for many minor ailments, and in some states are now allowed to prescribe birth control pills and other prescription drugs. Podiatrists perform minor surgery in their offices and chiropractors, massage therapists, clinical psychologists and others help patients manage the pain of chronic conditions as well as the stress of daily life. All of these providers can be paid with the tax-protected dollars of a Health Savings Account.

Another model of how to use alternatively skilled providers is found in the U.S. military. Millions of men and women have benefited over the years from the services of "corpsmen" and "corpswomen." In situations where medical problems occur with consistency, it is possible to train nonphysicians to perform patient care with high proficiency and reasonable costs. In many instances, these individuals return to civilian life in different careers, losing a valuable asset that could be integrated into the health care system. Whether winning a war in foreign nations or winning the war on health care costs, the training programs for military health care and the skilled personnel they produce could be used more effectively.

Because the medical treatment of disease provides immediate results and is thus more profitable for those in the "business" of health care, the physician shortage does not affect all practice areas equally. The greatest impact is on public health and preventive medicine, shown in Chapter 8 to have the greatest ability to improve longevity and reduce costs. "Physician extenders" work especially well in community-based education, testing, vaccination and wellness programs.

In the current system, third-party payers often require treatment in a physician's office to qualify for insurance reimbursement. In consumer driven health care, consumers allocate and spend their own health care dollars with the most efficient and effective providers from a wide range of specialties and qualifications. When cost reductions directly benefit patients, as is true with high deductible insurance policies and Health Savings Accounts, consumers will demand more of these well-trained but less expensive health care alternatives.

Increasing the Productivity of the Clinical Sector: Doing More with Less

The best solution to both the rising costs of direct patient care and the shortage of skilled labor is to increase productivity—delivering more patient care with fewer physicians and nurses. At the first mention of this idea, many readers probably grimace, counting the minutes after pushing a nurse call button or reading months-old magazines in physician waiting rooms, but such doesn't have to be the reality. Singapore achieves the highest quality of care in the world on nearly every objective measure with as few as 60 percent the number of physicians and nurses (per 100,000 patients) as the United States. The secret of increased productivity is working smarter, not harder.

Continual Process Improvement

The world's greatest companies, ranging from General Electric to Toyota, have long embraced continual process improvement as a way to lower costs, increase efficiency, and improve quality. Six Sigma is one such tool. By using statistical methods to determine how many defects occur in a process, managers can identify and eliminate the source of defects, eventually resulting in a process with zero defects. Today, thousands of workers have been trained in nearly every industry as Six Sigma "black belts" and various other shades of proficiency and such techniques have dramatically improved the productivity of U.S. companies. As leading health care institutions like the Mayo Clinic have learned, tools such as Six Sigma can also be a valuable weapon in the war on health costs, improving not only the efficiency of operations, but lowering the cost and improving clinical outcomes.

The concepts of Quality Assurance and Quality Improvement have their foundation in the 1950s writings of Dr. Edward Deming. Initially rejected in the United States, Deming's concepts found their greatest acceptance in Japan, leading to such quality advances and efficiency improvements that Japanese manufacturers gained enormous competitive advantage over the United States (most visibly in automobiles). Today, Toyota not only dominates the U.S. mid-size and luxury car markets, it is the world leader in quality and efficiency. When consumers begin spending their health care dollars with the most efficient and effective providers, it is inevitable that leading health care institutions will look to the same principles to survive and prevail in consumer driven health care.

Quality efforts work best when health care providers learn from one another. In the late 1980s, the Society of Thoracic Surgeons developed a database that is now used to set national standards for open heart surgery. In 1989, the New York State Department of Health mandated all open heart surgery cases be reviewed by a central agency, permitting today the publication of individual hospital and physician mortality rates in daily newspapers. Likewise, five hospitals in New England joined together to form the New England Study Group, visiting each other and learning from each other's techniques in surgeries and postoperative care. These information sharing efforts lowered the mortality rate and increased efficiency, achieving more uniform results among hospitals.

> *Solution to America's "Two Trillion Dollar Crisis": Health care and academic institutions should study, adopt and disseminate the continual quality improvement techniques from other industries, sharing best practices among all health care providers.*

A Failed Plan

In 1992, President Bill Clinton appointed his wife Hillary to create a task force studying health care problems, but she excluded most stakeholders in health care including large and small employers, the health insurance industry, physician and hospital groups, and pharmaceutical companies. As a defensive measure, the American Association of Physicians and Surgeons sued over the secrecy of Hillary's task force, revealing that it had exceeded its $300,000 budget by more than $10 million and had kept critical documents out of public view. Likewise, the Health Insurance Institute of America ran advertisements featuring "Harry and Louise," a middle-American husband and wife concerned that the Clinton plan would lead to "rationing of critical services, a loss of choice of doctors, and decreased quality of care." By the time the task force's 1,342–page plan was presented to Congress in 1993, support of consumers and lawmakers had waned and the bill failed without a vote.

The major shortcoming of the Clinton plan is that it attempted to achieve universal health coverage by requiring all employers to provide health insurance benefits for their workers. Because the government would mandate participation in heavily regulated health care purchasing alliances, 81 percent of companies polled "strongly agreed" the plan would create unnecessary government bureaucracy. Further, cost control caps on prices would have undermined market forces, possibly leading to critical shortages of health care services.

In consumer driven health care, the shortage of qualified health care professionals will not be solved by government edict but rather, as the institutions that train, license, and represent health care providers have the freedom to adapt to the needs of a rapidly changing market. Health care providers would be able to negotiate with consumers directly, setting fees at a level that provide sufficient incentive for quality care yet remain competitive enough to stay in business. As with other industries, consumers looking to maximize the value of their hard-earned savings (tucked away in their Health Savings Accounts) would "reward" efficient and effective caregivers with their business while "punishing" inefficient and ineffective caregivers by withholding funds. Because third-party payers would no longer set the rules, consumers would have greater leverage with lawmakers in pushing for policies funding scholarships for nursing and medical students, building programs for nursing and medical schools, and tort reform to lower malpractice insurance premiums.

Looking Toward the Future

The demand for direct patient care has no place to go but up. Add to that the increased costs that can be expected for cutting-edge pharmaceuticals, surgical techniques and medical devices, and it is clear that America faces even greater challenges in the future than in the past. If the nation fails to produce enough qualified physicians, nurses and other providers, the price of health care will soar to heights that will make America's "Two Trillion Dollar Crisis" a nostalgic memory of better times. That's why the supply problem must be addressed now, even though in the short run, costs may increase to increase the supply of skilled labor. Short term expenses, however, are actually long-term investments to decrease future costs. Some institutions are making the investments required to be the surviving institutions in ways described in the following chapter.

CHAPTER 6

The Inevitable Polarity of Health Care Delivery

"If you want to make enemies, change things."
—Woodrow Wilson

Disclaimer: *The following pages may be hazardous to your health. If you are an administrator, trustee, nurse, physician, or employee of a major general hospital, or are concerned about the future of health care providers in your community, the contents of this chapter may cause chronic anxiety, severe headaches, gastrointestinal indigestion, and possibly depression. Only individuals desiring better health care for lower costs should read this chapter.*

If you want to see what will happen in the future to health care providers, just look at the airline, steel, or auto industries. The same trends followed by these industries, as well as department stores, booksellers (or most any retailer), accounting firms, and banks will occur in health care as consumers pay a greater share of their own health care costs. The institutional life cycle, inevitable in all industries, is a predictable pattern.

When a consumer need is identified, firms go into business to meet that need and an industry develops. During the growth phase, firms develop products, establish customer service, and accumulate capital. Competition appears as firms differentiate themselves from other firms doing the same types of things. The most efficient firms with the best marketing increase sales while the least efficient are either acquired by their more efficient counterparts or, unable to compete, go out of business. According to Jagdish Sheth and Rajendra Sisodia, authors of *Rule of Three* (Free Press, 2002), industries in the mature stage evolve to three dominant competitors accompanied by a few smaller specialty firms appealing to niche markets. In this universal phenomenon, the three largest firms begin to look alike, offering similar products and services, and serving customers in similar ways with similar cost structures.

The story does not end here, however, as the large dominant firms with commodity offerings are eventually attacked and displaced by small, innovative competitors that keep costs low, services minimal, and serve segments too small to be attractive to major firms. Examples of this creative destruction process are described in Dr. Clayton Christenson's classic book, *The Innovator's Dilemma* (Harvard Business Press, 1997). There should be no question as to *whether* the normal institutional life cycle applies to health care providers. The unanswered questions are *when* changes will occur, and *who* the dominant players will be.

The study of institutional life cycles is critical to understanding the types of health care providers that will prosper when health care is subject to the discipline of consumer-driven markets. Low cost, mass providers of health care will grow, but so also will those offering limited services appealing to specialized market niches. If hospitals and other health care providers "in the middle" don't find ways to become more efficient, they will find it difficult to survive.

Polarity of Trade

Polarity of trade describes the phenomena of the "shrinking middle," or when the only successful business models are those that provide basic services at a low cost to the masses or highly specialized services to selected niche markets.

As a child, do you remember going downtown to a large department store during the holidays, gazing in awe and wonder at the lights and decorations before telling Santa which of the many toys on display you wanted for Christmas? In Los Angeles, you might have gone to Bullock's, in Philadelphia to John Wanamaker, or in Cleveland to Higbee's (icon of *A Christmas Story*). Nearly every major city had at least one department store that was all things to all people. Go to those same stores today, however, and you won't find any toys. In many cities, you won't even find the department store—just an abandoned building or vacant lot.

Department stores, like many other middle-of-the-market retailers, went the way of dinosaurs because they were prey for what Harvard Business Professor Malcolm McNair called "The Wheel of Retailing." This process involves innovative, specialized retailers entering markets to compete against large, established stores with broad product lines. Retail profitability is determined by a combination of margin and turns. Whereas traditional department stores have high overhead and attain only moderate sales volume on their large inventories, the new competitors carry a limited number of items and sell them in large quantities, providing not only higher turns, but also higher margins due to volume discounts and a more efficient supply chain. When department stores could no longer match the low prices offered by these new entrants, consumers began to leave in favor of stores like Wal-Mart, Costco, and Home Depot.

In the United States, the greatest sales growth is found among mass retailers offering low prices based on high efficiency, but there is also growth among specialty stores who find riches in the niches. Having a little something for everyone means traditional department stores don't have much of anything for consumers looking for something special. Niche market segments are willing to pay a premium for the wide assortment of colors, sizes, and styles found at specialty stores such as Chico's, Victoria's Secret, and Pottery Barn. Although a few traditional department stores, such as Milwaukee-based Kohl's, have become efficient enough to compete against the new mass retailers, and others such as Seattle-based Nordstrom have carved out a niche focusing on exclusive brands and superior customer service, most have not changed fast enough to survive the shrinking big middle. Expect the same trends in health care delivery once consumers pay an increasing share of the cost in consumer driven health care.

Hospitals and physicians' offices basically are retailers of health care products and services, subject to the same consumer-driven trends and demands as any other retailer. If you are an administrator, trustee, nurse, physician, or employee of a large general hospital, ask yourself the following questions: Are we a Wal-Mart, Costco, or Home Depot, or are we a Bullock's, Wanamaker's or Higbee's? Are we a Chico's, Victoria's Secret, or Pottery Barn, or are we a Kohl's or Nordstrom? In the future, some of today's large general hospitals will still exist, but in far more efficient forms and without their "toy departments." Others will be converted to retirement homes, specialized care facilities (perhaps for Alzheimer's patients) or, like some department stores, just boarded up.

High Fliers

The airline industry is in a crisis as crunching as health care. In recent years, TWA folded, United and US Airways entered bankruptcy, and American and Delta have been fighting to avoid Chapter 11. Yet one airline has been profitable for 31 years straight, has loyal employees who enjoy their work and are also union members, and receives the highest levels of satisfaction in consumer polls. Its name is Southwest and its stock symbol says much about the reason for its success— LUV. JetBlue Airways has the same basic business model with the added advantage of newer aircraft equipped with in-seat television.

Can quality be achieved by low cost firms? Southwest and JetBlue are prototypes for innovative forms of health care delivery that can be expected to emerge, grow and threaten the existing health care infrastructure. These airlines demonstrate that low cost providers can offer higher consumer satisfaction than traditional, high cost, full service firms. Consider the following ranking of airline quality using 15 attributes considered important to consumers:

1. JetBlue Airways
2. Alaska Airlines
3. Southwest Airlines
4. America West
5. US Airways
6. Northwest Airlines
7. Continental Airlines
8. AirTran
9. United Airlines
10. ATA
11. American Airlines
12. Delta Air Lines

Source: University of Nebraska at Omaha Aviation Institute and W. Frank Barton School of Business at Wichita State University

Three of the top four airlines are low cost carriers, with JetBlue achieving the best overall performance. These airlines are gobbling up market share from traditional network carriers because they're on time more often, bump fewer passengers, mishandle fewer bags and generate fewer customer service complaints. Granted, nobody wants to cut costs in hospitals if it compromises patient safety, but safety is also a given for the airlines. With newer aircraft and more focused processes, low cost airlines actually have safety records as good as or better than their high cost counterparts. Wouldn't you likewise want health care from the hospital that performs the services you need more reliably, with less waiting and fewer mistakes?

To solve America's "Two Trillion Dollar Crisis," costs must be removed from traditional health care delivery systems. Examining how airlines lowered costs and raised standards reveals what consumers will also demand of hospitals when they start paying an increasing share of the bill. In 2004, here are the costs to fly one seat one mile at various U.S. airlines:

US Airways	11.8 cents
Alaska	10.63
Northwest	10.61
Delta	10.32
United	9.83
American	9.50
Continental	9.42
AirTran	8.46
Frontier	8.09
Southwest	8.09
America West	7.72
JetBlue	5.90

Source: *Wall Street Journal,* August 12, 2004, p. A1

The salient point is that the *best* service is achieved by the airlines with the *lowest* costs. JetBlue and Southwest reduce costs by cross-training workers to perform jobs other than their primary responsibility (rather than sitting idle between flights, flight attendants also check passengers in at the gate), and flying newer and more fuel-efficient aircraft with cutting-edge avionics. They also utilize tighter financial controls, better scheduling of supply to match demand (resulting in higher seat occupancy), and proprietary reservation systems that avoid costly travel agent commissions. Traditional airlines, by contrast, typically have older workers who expect high salaries with guaranteed annual pay increases and gold-plated pensions, rigid work rules locked in by heritage union contracts, hub-and-spoke networks based more on history than current demand, older airplanes that are less fuel efficient and less flexible to new routes, large amounts of debt, and many costly amenities (city ticket offices, club rooms, in-flight meals, etc.). Apply to health care what has occurred with airlines and it becomes clear which kinds of hospitals won't survive in the future.

Consumer driven health care will challenge today's health care providers with new competitors that provide a higher quality of service yet operate at a lower cost. Implementing the same types of strategies and processes found at Southwest and JetBlue, these innovative firms will omit amenities not valued by consumers, provide more efficient scheduling of patients and procedures, greater cross-training of employees, newer and more efficient diagnostic technology, equity financing by management (including physicians), locations based on customer convenience, and cash (or credit card) payment instead of expensive insurance reimbursement schemes.

> *Solution to America's "Two Trillion Dollar Crisis": When consumers pay a greater share of their own health care costs, they will choose highly efficient low-cost providers based on the business models of Southwest Airlines and JetBlue Airways, instead of traditional general hospitals.*

Superefficient Retailers as Models for Superefficient Hospitals

Firms that change their operations at the strategic level will not only be most successful in the polarity of trade, but many will achieve victory before their competitors even realize the threat. Once traditional, high cost firms finally understand the strategic advantages enjoyed by new, superefficient competitors, they are often too far behind to adapt. Two retail examples, Aldi and Wal-Mart, illustrate how new entrants to consumer markets became so efficient that they won the battle before industry leaders realized what was happening.

Do You Aldi?

At most chain supermarkets, consumers pay $3.50 to $4.50 for a box of breakfast cereal but at Aldi, the same product costs $.89 to $1.29. Because Aldi's shorter supply chain provides inventory turns five to 10 times greater than traditional supermarkets, the product is also fresher and should keep longer.

If you are an affluent reader of this book, you may not know much about Aldi, even though its owners, brothers Theo and Karl Albrecht, have a personal net worth of $34 billion, making them third richest in the world according to *Forbes* ranking (2005). Founded in Germany, Aldi, short for "Albrecht Discount," is one of the largest supermarket chains in the world with 4,000 stores in 11 countries. From an 800–store footprint that extends from New York to Colorado, Aldi is also quickly expanding in the United States.

The reasons for Aldi's radically low prices are expense control, inventory velocity, and supply chain management. Aldi saves consumers 30 to 40 percent over many competitors by using SKU (Stock Keeping Unit) simplification, which is carrying an assortment of the highest volume items instead of multiple brands, sizes, and package types of the same basic product. Aldi is a Spartan atmosphere and marketing functions are shifted to the most efficient providers, which in many instances are consumers. It doesn't take credit cards or checks, it doesn't provide free paper or plastic bags, and it requires a 25–cent deposit on shopping carts (refunded when the cart is returned), reducing drastically the overhead incurred by higher priced competitors. Rather than stocking shelves, pallets of goods are arranged by forklift trucks, where consumers pick products directly from boxes. When the boxes are empty, consumers use them to carry home their groceries—saving the costs of both waste recycling and new shopping bags. Suppliers also don't have to pay "slotting" allowances or absorb costs of returns and credits that drive up prices at traditional retailers. Could health care providers achieve a similar level of efficiency by providing basic services in a low overhead environment and shifting some tasks to consumers?

Just because Aldi's overhead is the industry's lowest, doesn't mean it skimps on its people. Aldi pays its cashiers $3 to 4 more per hour than competitors and in 2004, college graduates received a starting salary of $62,000 for management training positions—nearly twice what competitors pay. That's an important point to consider because it's sometimes naively assumed that high salaries of physicians and nurses lead to high prices for consumers. As Aldi demonstrates, when higher salaries result in higher productivity, they still yield lower prices for consumers and profits as high as 9.5 percent versus one to three percent for major chains.

Simplicity is the key to Aldi's success. Aldi knows what items consumers want, it keeps overhead low, and organizes its supply chain to achieve the prices consumers are willing to pay (instead of what suppliers want to charge). If you are not familiar with Aldi, we suggest that you visit a location near you. But don't reach for the Yellow Pages—Aldi stores are unlisted to save the cost of advertising and answering incoming calls. Instead, locations and hours are listed online. Once you discover how to reduce your grocery bill by a hundred or more dollars a month, you might even become one of its fans.

Consumers who have lots of money to pay for groceries may prefer the greater selection and ambiance of high priced stores over Aldi's appeal to frugality. But when most consumers are given a choice between withdrawing from the family's Health Savings Account (HSA) to pay $25 for quality medical services in a Spartan environment that does not accept insurance (cash or credit card only) and a doctor's office with all the frills for $70, which will consumers choose? As long as "someone else" is paying, there is no reason to choose the low cost alternative, but when the money comes out of their wallet or HSA, it can safely be forecast that a substantial segment of consumers will turn from frills to frugality.

Do You "Get" Wal-Mart?

Wall Street analysts didn't understand the appeal of Wal-Mart until it was too late to take advantage of the rapid growth that made millionaires of its early investors and employees. With a customer base primarily in the rural South and Midwest, a lot of urban consumers shake their heads and say, "I just don't get it." But the 82 percent of Americans who shop at Wal-Mart each year (100 million customers each week) do "get it!" They know they always find low prices and shelves more likely to be stocked than competitors like K-Mart that creak along with antiquated logistics systems. They know that when Wal-Mart builds a Super Center in their town, grocery prices drop about 14 percent at other stores, racking up millions of dollars in savings—even for consumers who shop elsewhere. Clearly Wal-Mart is doing something right. Its sales are more than a quarter trillion dollars and analysts project it to be a trillion-dollar company within a decade.

Wal-Mart is successful because it passes its savings from improved efficiency back to the consumer. With superior expense and inventory control, Wal-Mart operates with overhead costs in the 16 to 17 percent range, compared to industry averages of 20 to 23 percent. Although Wal-Mart has tremendous purchasing power, even when it pays suppliers the same wholesale price as competitors, consumers still get lower prices because of the more efficient supply chain. That's why Wal-Mart's competitors often require vendors to sell them products slightly different—in packaging, size, or other attributes—than what is sold at Wal-Mart.

Another lesson to be learned from Wal-Mart is from its strategy of building facilities where costs are lowest and competition weakest. When fighting a war, it's usually fatal to launch a frontal attack at the core of a superior force. Flanking strategies work best. Wal-Mart didn't originally attack the chain department stores and grocery retailers that dominated urban areas, but rather, built its strength in small towns where costs were low and competitors backward, gradually circling cities until it was ready to enter the suburbs and today, large cities. Eventually, the strategy gave Wal-Mart the ability to take on (and beat) stores like K-Mart, Sears and Montgomery Ward. Would the Mayo Clinic be as successful if it were in Chicago or New York as it is in Rochester, Minnesota? New forms of health care providers will follow the same strategy to conquer many of the entrenched players—starting in lower cost and underserved areas and building strength until they have the scale to attack high cost traditional general hospitals.

Entrepreneurial forms of health care will probably be successful to the degree they follow the same formula as Wal-Mart:

- Gain a foothold in markets others don't serve and attack big markets later
- Create a culture and a message to explain to consumers and employees who you are and what you stand for
- Emphasize the products, prices and experiences that consumers value and prefer over others
- Add a little magic to the brand value of the consumer experience
- Listen to and observe consumers and change accordingly
- Change the infrastructure and systems to fit the wants and needs of customers instead of hanging onto historic practices

Can traditional general hospitals survive in a consumer-driven environment? The growing polarity of business organizations is disruptive to existing organizations, but inevitable. The airline, steel, and automobile industries prove overcapacity never goes away easily or painlessly. However, *it does go away* when consumers make choices reflecting their own preferences and pocketbooks.

Although the United States has yet to experience large-scale examples of low cost, streamlined, highly efficient health care delivery models offering minimum frills and high value to consumers, innovators around the country are testing the waters. Large health care providers like Kaiser Permanente, Duke University Health System, and Intermountain Health Care have adopted some of the management, logistics and location strategies of superefficient organizations in other industries. Many private physicians no longer accept patients who require the high administrative costs of filing insurance claims, practicing on a cash-only basis and passing on the savings to consumers.

One innovator, Minnesota-based MinuteClinic, claims to have treated more than 150,000 patients since the company began operations in 2000 and has achieved a 99 percent customer satisfaction rating. As of publication, MinuteClinic operated 13 clinics located in retail stores, shopping centers, and corporate offices in the Minneapolis-St. Paul Metro area. However, through a 2004 alliance with Target Stores, MinuteClinic is rapidly expanding into new markets such as Baltimore, Maryland. Common ailments, which can be diagnosed with a brief history, physical examination, and perhaps an x-ray or lab test, are treated on the spot. MinuteClinics are staffed primarily by nurse practitioners and physician's assistants, and true to its slogan, "you're sick, we're quick," its fees are half that of a traditional doctor's office. Prescriptions can even be filled at the adjacent Target pharmacy, a time-saving convenience.

Although MinuteClinic originally required patients to pay cash at the time of service, employees were so satisfied with the experience that they began demanding MinuteClinic as an in-network benefit and today, nearly all health plans in Minnesota provide access to MinuteClinic. In addition, some large employers opened Minute-Clinics within their corporate facilities exclusively for their employees—such as at the Best Buy corporate headquarters in suburban Richfield, Minnesota. Since MinuteClinic's inception, the company has saved uninsured individuals, self-insured employers, and health insurance companies more than $7 million and countless hours of wasted time. It's efficient, accurate, and reduces the costs of health care delivery, which is quite appealing when consumers can bank the savings in their HSAs.

Frugal, no-frills quality medicine is a proven concept in other countries, as illustrated by Chapter 3. Just like Aldi and Southwest Airlines, innovators in health care who provide quality care, without the frills and at prices consumers are willing to pay, will not only find a profitable niche, they will also affect the viability of all other health care institutions in consumer driven health care. So, who will be the Herb Kelleher, Albrecht Brothers, or Sam Walton, to build a system for low cost, high quality hospital care? Ten years from now, you'll probably see his or her picture on the cover of major business magazines and medical journals.

The Plight of the General Hospital

Hospitals have two sets of "end users"—patients and physicians. Many patients have no choice as to which hospital they use, going either where their physician is on the staff, or to the closest as a matter of need. Despite problems such as large numbers of uninsured patients who use the emergency room for primary care because no low cost, no-frills alternative exists and because they lack the knowledge to practice the "DIY" medicine found in other nations, most hospitals still serve patients well.

Physicians, however, are more likely to have a choice between referring their patients to a hospital, a specialized facility, and treating them in the office. General hospitals that don't—or can't—provide favorable working conditions will lose the ability to serve patients well. Heritage locations in declining urban areas, far from growing suburbs and with limited parking, are unattractive to employees in a tight labor market. In some practices such as internal or family medicine, a physician may have only one patient in the hospital at any given time. If driving and parking take more time than seeing the patient, many physicians won't make the trip, relying instead on "hospitalists" (physicians who practice only in the hospital) to treat patients. Because physicians are customers rather than partners with the hospital, their objectives are not always consistent with those of the hospital. Sometimes an adversarial relationship develops between hospital administrators and physicians, each looking after their own best interests.

In the third-party payer system, an open heart procedure performed with no complications on a patient admitted on an outpatient basis costs about $24,000 with about $2,000 going to the surgeon, $2,000 to the anesthesiologist and $20,000 in hospital fees—meaning the surgeon who referred the business to the hospital and performed the operation collects less than 10 percent of all the fees charged for the hospital admission! In other surgical specialties, such as orthopedics, similar ratios prevail, a key to understanding why institutional medicine will be turned upside down as consumer driven health care creates an open market where physicians and consumers can negotiate the most favorable terms, without the mandates of some distant third-party payer.

Increased competition from outpatient surgical centers, freestanding image centers, specialty hospitals, and even doctors' offices, is diverting previous revenue from cash-strapped general hospitals. Colonoscopies, MRI scans, cataract surgery, and other profitable procedures are moving to community based medical offices, usually in suburban locations that are more convenient for physicians and patients. Not only do smaller offices incur less overhead, they're also more sensitive to the needs of consumers and physicians.

Because hospitals have seen growth in the total number of outpatient surgeries (as opposed to market share), many have simply not noticed the threat posed by these other delivery channels. The plight

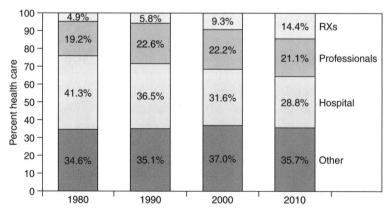

Exhibit 6.1   Percentage Distribution of Health Care Expenditures U.S. (1980–2010)

of general hospitals is illustrated in Figure 6.1, which shows their percentage of total health care expenditures dropping from 41.3 percent in 1980 to 31.6 percent in 2000 and forecast to be 28.8 percent in 2010. With physician competition likely to intensify, general hospitals that want to survive must consider local needs and cultivate working relationships with doctors.

In physician-owned hospitals, physicians get a return on their investment in addition to their professional fees, putting administrators and physicians on the same team and directly aligning them with hospital goals. The same alignment exists in hospitals where physicians receive performance-based incentives based on improving hospital efficiency. To align their goals, a hospital must become such an integral part of a physician's practice that the physician cannot practice medicine without it. Unfortunately, with margins of one to three percent, many general hospitals lack the capital needed to update their plants or buy new, more expensive medical devices that would help physicians do their jobs better.

Polarity leaves firms that try to be all things to all people in great difficulty. Without the low prices necessary to attract mass markets or the specialized services that appeal to market niches willing and able to pay premium prices, the plight of general hospitals is not much different than the plight of department stores. Many general hospitals are losing money and others are headed toward bankruptcy, but as long as "someone else" is paying the health care costs of most consumers, there is little incentive for the model to change. When consumers pay a large portion of health care out of their own wallets, however, they will accelerate the shift to more efficient delivery models. Short of increased subsidies from government, community, or charitable sources, only the best managed, most efficient—and perhaps most paranoid—general hospitals will survive.

The Case for Specialty Hospitals

Specialty hospitals, which treat certain medical problems or perform limited procedures including maternity, orthopedics and heart procedures, are growing rapidly growing across the country because they provide higher quality at a lower cost. "Practice makes perfect" and repeating the same procedures over and over results in better patient outcomes with reduced complications (affecting morbidity/mortality rates) and shorter hospital stays. Concentrated patient volume also allows cutting-edge technology and procedures to be integrated more rapidly and at a lower cost per use.

According to the General Accounting Office, a specialty hospital is one in which at least two-thirds of inpatient insurance claims are in one or two major diagnosis categories, or those in which two-thirds or more are surgical. Exceptions are hospitals owned by the government and those for rehabilitation, psychiatry, alcohol and drug treatment, and children. Specialty hospitals nationally are concentrated in areas where state law does not restrict hospital development and about two-thirds are concentrated in seven states. At least 28 states have at least one specialty hospital.

Because every member of the specialty hospital team is focused on a narrow range of maladies, there is greater opportunity for team members to share innovations while the organization focuses on the patient experience, calming patients' fears and perhaps providing a more homelike atmosphere. In the smaller facility, physicians are likely to have greater control over patient care, with the ability to make the most informed decisions. When physicians are investors, they are motivated to see that patients receive the best care, leaving not just satisfied with the outcome, but delighted with the total experience.

A major reason for the growth of specialty hospitals is that physicians have an opportunity to earn more money because of greater efficiency. Instead of commuting to a difficult parking location, fighting elevators and procedures over which they have no control, and waiting for patient transfers between departments, physicians can schedule time more productively. When turnaround times from one case to the next are minimal, physicians can see more patients each day. Malpractice insurance premiums are also lower with greater experience. And the ability to see their investment increase in value provides an incentive for attracting the best physicians.

The Case Against Specialty Hospitals

Opposition to specialty hospitals is based on allegations that they "cream-skim" patients who are the healthiest and most able to pay, assuring favorable outcomes and the greatest profits. In general hospitals, the ability to treat Medicaid patients with below market reimbursements and indigent patients with high uncollectible receivables depends on the cross-subsidization of successful, high margin practices. If specialty hospitals siphon profitable cardiac and orthopedic patients, which produce the highest percent of revenue for general hospitals, the ability to provide critical but often unprofitable services including emergency rooms, burn units, and intensive care could be undermined. For example, Although 92 percent of general hospitals have emergency rooms (the "gateway" for Medicaid and underinsured patients), they are in less than half of all specialty hospitals. Another complaint is that specialty hospitals hire away experienced nurses and technical personnel, leaving general hospitals to replace them with inexperienced graduates.

These allegations are disputed, however, by studies demonstrating that specialty hospitals see patients whose conditions are just as severe as those seen by general hospitals. Also, where specialty hospitals have entered direct competition with general hospitals, general hospitals have adapted to the change, in some cases by providing more competitive offerings. Specialty hospitals have pushed general hospitals to make improvements including extending operating room hours, improving scheduling, and upgrading equipment. Despite their naysayers, specialty hospitals have not dismantled the health care system nor have they forced traditional general hospitals to cut critical services or charity care.

For decades, "someone else" besides the patient determined which health care facilities were used. That's changing. When consumers pay more of the cost themselves, a new "decider" about specialty-general hospital debates emerges. It's you, the consumer.

Case Study: It's NASH, not M.A.S.H!

To glimpse the future for specialty hospitals, we conclude this chapter with a case study illustrating future directions in the polarity of health care delivery, and how shifting functions to more efficient providers leads to lower costs and higher quality. The case is named NASH, not the car, but a specialty hospital in New Albany, a modern, carefully designed suburb on the northeast perimeter of Columbus, Ohio.

The New Albany Surgical Hospital (NASH) is about as different in appearance from M.A.S.H. (the movie-popularized Mobile Army Surgical Hospitals of the Korean War era) as it is similar in focused function. Unlike M.A.S.H. units that were often housed in tents, the spatial NASH building with its distinctive Georgian architecture is located just minutes from the airport and Interstate 270, providing ready access not only to the 1.5 million residents of greater Columbus, but also patients across the region.

Happenstance? Hardly. An old adage says the three most important attributes of successful retailing are: location, location, and location. It is a principle no less important in designing better health care organizations than designing a successful shopping center. Easton Town Center, a lifestyle center that innovatively combines entertainment, shopping and dining experiences is located nearby. This makes it possible to schedule surgery at NASH and put the family in a comfortable Hilton hotel where they can occupy their time shopping at Nordstrom and celebrating a successful surgery with dinner at Cheesecake Factory, Smith & Wollensky, Max & Erma's or any of the other outstanding restaurants nearby.

Although celebrating a surgery is hardly on the mind of any patient, a specialty hospital is designed to engender peace of mind. From medical, technical, and logistical perspectives, specialty hospitals enhance the patient experience. Engineered to deliver short stays with no complications and quick rehabilitations—NASH aims for an overall celebratory experience.

NASH has a total of eight operating rooms (ORs) that are divided in two pods of four. Architects reserved plenty of space for low cost and easy future expansion, and for maximum efficiency, situating all equipment and supplies in the center of each pod. Instead of the typical eight-foot wide hospital corridors, NASH's are ten-feet wide, offering a fast and easy flow of patients, staff and materials.

Surgeons have a separate parking lot and a private entrance that gives them immediate access to a changing room, scrub area and OR pod. Eliminate elevators, parking and other hassles, and time surgeries precisely—with few chances to modify the schedule—and it is possible to reduce a surgeon's nonproductive time by three hours or more a day. Multiply that several times by the efficiencies achieved by all the other staff, and it is easy to see why specialty hospitals have the potential to reduce America's health care costs and give general (all-purpose) hospitals a run for their money.

Further adding to the satisfaction and speedy recovery of patients are the forty-eight specially designed rooms and bathrooms that match closely the needs of the muscular-skeletal surgery on which

NASH is focused. At NASH, every room is private and larger than those of most hospitals. The tables, chairs and beds are ortho-elevated and the bathrooms have elevated commodes, roll-in showers, shower seats and other features designed to permit immediate rehabilitation and physical therapy in the patient room rather than remote, less accessible locations. Patient transport expense, which accounts for 15 percent of costs in traditional general hospitals, is nearly nonexistent. Instead of having to order supplies from a central repository, at NASH supplies (and some pharmaceuticals) are stored in locked cabinets in patient rooms, accessible to staff. All rooms are equipped with keyboard-empowered televisions, providing patients and families access to their email and the Internet. In-room dining is similar to hotel room service, allowing the patient to choose when and what to eat, adding to the experience of patients and families. This service also costs less than the staffing and facilities required by hospitals that try to serve all patients at the same time.

NASH exemplifies function shifting. Who's better able to know how a patient wants pillows fluffed, or when the patient wants a beverage, or when a patient wants to order food from the hospital food service or a nearby restaurant? Is it accompanying family members or a nurse? Who can perform this function most economically? At NASH, patient rooms are equipped with "sleeper" chairs for family members. The comfortable surgical waiting room at NASH is equipped with a computer station providing instantaneous information from the OR and other hospital areas. Or, if the family wants to leave, the information provider can call their cell phone with updates. If the family doesn't have a cell phone, NASH loans them one. It's likely some families will be in the dining area because it is inviting, served from the central kitchen that also serves patients and staff, and opens to a patio environment where families or staff sip their favorite Starbucks drinks. When hospitals are designed and built upon the principle of shifting essential functions to the most efficient caregiver, everyone wins—the patient, the family, the medical staff, and whoever is paying the bill.

Innovative forms of specialty hospitals now emerging with consumer driven health care will eventually force more efficiency into existing hospitals, partly due to their advantage of a late start in technology. Examine the corridors of many hospitals and you'll see physicians and staff carrying patients' charts in manual form. After rounds, the orders may be given to nurses and sometime—often quite a long time—the orders may be administered. At NASH, orders are entered into the physician's digital assistant, transmitted immediately to the appropriate station or person, and are on their way to being implemented before the physician has completed patient visits. And it's wireless—a huge savings over hard-wired environments.

If you have experienced a stay in a hospital, you probably know that one of the most perplexing questions is when and how to talk to a doctor. There are always doctors somewhere in the hospital, of course, but who is the appropriate one—an ER doctor, a surgeon, or one of many other specialists? Is it a primary care or "family" physician who struggles to make time available in both hospital and office settings? And what's the likelihood the physician is available at the same time a spouse or other family member is present? For surgical patients such as those at NASH, the physician needed to see a patient after surgery might likely be an internal medicine specialist able to treat other problems that the patient may have—diabetes, cardiovascular issues, infections or other issues less directly related to the surgery. NASH solves this problem by maintaining an internist in the hospital on a 24–hour basis. The level of care, amount of information and patient satisfaction is higher than in the traditional hospital environment by transferring these functions to specialized personnel and technology.

The Internet-equipped TVs in patient rooms exist for much more than entertainment. They also access the learning center, allowing patients and staff to view educational materials designed to help them understand health care and facilitate recovery and rehabilitation. Need to see how to do a physical therapy routine? The information is just a click away from every patient or staff member.

Visit physician and staff areas and conference rooms and you'll also see state-of-the-art plasma screen monitors, connected by camera to operating rooms and other areas essential to communication and educational processes. A physician can be performing a surgery or delivering a PowerPoint-assisted lecture connected to residents, staff or other physicians—who can ask questions with their own camera—in a conference room outside the OR. And the conference room doesn't need to be just for those at NASH; it can easily be connected to other hospitals in Columbus, or almost as readily, in New York or Los Angeles. These video-equipped conference rooms are the core of the learning center for all staff members at NASH and large enough to bring together every member of the staff for important personal or video meetings (and large enough to serve holiday parties and other team-building functions).

Excellent surgeons and excellent facilities are not the whole story, however, of why specialty hospitals are changing the American health care system. The "rest of the story," as radio commentator Paul Harvey likes to say, is about the kind of staff possible with specialty hospitals. This part of the story may ultimately be the most important attribute of specialty hospitals. It's built on the same principle contained in Hal Rosenbaum's book, *The Customer Comes Second* (HarperBusiness, 2002) and built into the philosophies of firms such as Johnson & Johnson, Marriott Hotels and Wal-Mart, recognizing that it's difficult to take care of customers well, if employees are not taken care as well as (or even better than) the customers.

NASH doesn't have "employees" but rather, "team members" who are closely focused on special problems—spine and joint surgery—in an organization small enough such that every team member can know every other team member. To help the process, color coded uniforms immediately identify areas of responsibility. A concierge helps team members arrange household help, tickets to community events, and even dry cleaning. The human resources department helps team members learn how to do their jobs better and understand that no one job is more important than any other. Everyone's purpose is to understand and provide the best care possible, of course, but there is also a focus on understanding the nature of the specialty hospital business and how team members' own performance contributes to efficient and profitable operation of the facility. The process goes beyond just performing their jobs for their own benefits, but rather, improving the entire community. High morale, a belief in what they do, and constantly improving skill in providing care; that's the ultimate path to providing better health care and lower costs that accompany low turnover. The goal of human resources is simple—"to make this the best place you've ever worked."

With such advantages to patients, team members and the cost of health care, it might be assumed that everyone would welcome specialty hospitals such as NASH. That's hardly been the case. Nationwide, specialty hospital foes have been successful in lobbying for special taxes on outpatient surgical hospitals, laboratories and imaging centers, requirements that specialty hospitals operate 24–hour emergency rooms, or (in the case of Florida) just banning specialty hospitals altogether. NASH was started by a few visionary physicians who invested time, energy and money to bring the concept to reality with the remaining investment by Specialty Medical, a Nashville-based firm that provides administrative services for the facility. Although the concept was originally proposed as a product extension to two of the major health care systems in Columbus, both declined. Some competing local hospitals later banned doctors at NASH from performing procedures at the hospitals where they used to work and the state of Ohio has proposed legislation prohibiting physicians from referring patients to specialty hospitals in which they have a financial interest. These developments also make the NASH case instructive for understanding the conflicts likely to occur in reforming the American health care system.

A Concluding Perspective on Polarity

Will many of America's general hospitals turn into the Montgomery Wards, John Wanamaker's, or K-Marts of the future? Time will tell, but when consumer driven health care creates an open market for health care services, consumers will migrate to the most effective and efficient providers and physicians will work for those that provide the greatest opportunities for ownership and advancement. The most successful health care providers will learn from case examples in other industries such as Southwest Airlines and Aldi, while others will study innovative health care models like NASH.

The M.A.S.H hospitals of movie and TV fame were not fancy (often little more than a tent) but they were focused. And they housed a cohesive team of people almost fanatically dedicated to a single purpose—immediate care of combat injuries. Whether the health care model for America in the future is NASH, M.A.S.H, or Mayo Clinic, institutions that achieve alignment of their mission and medical staff to be focused on consumer-driven needs, it can safely be predicted, will be winners in the inevitable polarity of health care delivery.

CHAPTER 7

How a Health Savings Account Fights the Evils of First Dollar Coverage

"It takes as much energy to wish as it does to plan."
Eleanor Roosevelt

Imagine a world in which consumers purchased all of life's necessities the same way that Americans currently purchase health care. If, for example, people believed having a job entitled them to walk into any store (or restaurant), select whatever food they "needed," and "pay" for it by presenting their "food insurance" card? All charges would be sent to an insurance company for approval and reimbursement. Of course, the insurance company would grapple with tough questions like whether a late-night latte charged at Starbucks is "nutritionally necessary." Food prices would rise to cover these administrative costs and provide a profit for the insurance company. To cut costs, the insurance company might begin to restrict choices, requiring consumers to shop across town or eat only on certain days of the week. Or, it could deny reimbursement altogether. Sound ridiculous? It's fundamentally the same way Americans are used to purchasing health care in the current third-party payer system.

Whether it is food, clothing, or travel, when consumers make their own decisions about what they need and pay for it themselves, they force firms to give them what they want at prices they are willing to pay. Should buying health care be any different? When two stores charge different prices for the same product, consumers normally migrate to the cheaper store, which prospers and grows while the higher priced competitor eventually goes out of business. If, however, a "food insurance" card reimbursed purchases at both stores, there would be no impetus for consumers to choose the more efficient seller, allowing inefficient providers to coexist with efficient providers, and thus, raising total costs. Because consumers control their own food purchases, both the proportion of U.S. GDP devoted to food costs and the proportion of consumer income spent on food has dropped continuously for many decades, resulting in not only the most efficient food supply and distribution system in the world, but also one that provides a high level of quality, selection, and safety.

At first glance, the free market system may seem to favor the affluent because not everyone can afford to buy food at the most attractive supermarkets and restaurants. Those with limited incomes become wise shoppers, perhaps scouring Aldi, Wal-Mart, and dollar stores for bargains. They stretch their dollars by eating spaghetti instead of steak and choosing White Castle over white tablecloths.

In the most drastic circumstances, some people don't even have money for food, relying instead on government assistance or eating at soup kitchens. These Americans are all in the same position as people without health insurance. Fortunately, most Americans don't have to rely on soup kitchens, but discussing them is important because when consumers are uninsured, many hospitals now refuse treatment except for emergencies. In fact, some doctors flatly refuse Medicaid patients because reimbursements are less than the cost of processing the required paperwork. Even patients who can afford their own health care may be concerned that costs are rising faster than their budgets can handle.

When decision-making for health care is shifted from "someone else" (third-party payers) to consumers, there are three consequences:

1. Consumers understand the prices they are paying and learn to make choices that give the most value for limited budgets
2. Consumers reward firms that do the best job of meeting their expectations for price, service, and quality, causing efficient, well-managed firms to grow and prosper and inefficient firms to exit the market
3. The economic system operates efficiently in the creation and allocation of scarce resources

While consumers have long been in the driver's seat for food purchases, when it comes to health care, they still rely on "someone else" to tell them what to buy. Except for laser eye surgery and cosmetic surgery, for which competition has driven prices down and quality up, consumers often don't put much effort into understanding the product they are buying, whether it's the best solution to their problem, or what competitors charge. Moreover, so long as "someone else" pays most of the bills, there is little economic incentive to change any of these behaviors. Many of these problems are the evils of first dollar coverage in typical health insurance plans.

Good Insurance versus Bad Insurance

What is "good" insurance? The answer may be found in any insurance textbook: *the purpose of insurance is to manage risk by transferring large, uncertain losses to small, certain losses.*

The risk that a parent in his or her twenties or thirties will die is low, but should it occur, the effect on the surviving spouse and children could be devastating. Without the extra income, the family may be unable to meet its financial obligations. To reduce these consequences, the young family can purchase term life insurance with a large face amount—perhaps a million dollars—for a small premium of a few hundred dollars annually, based on the policyholder's age and health risk. Every family in the insurance pool loses a little something each year—the premium—but the family that has a large, catastrophic loss gains the face amount of the policy. That's good insurance.

Insurance that pays for small, frequent losses expected to occur routinely is bad insurance. For example, auto insurance usually has a deductible to cover the nicks and bumps most drivers experience that produce frequent, relatively small losses. Although these losses can be predicted, if they were insured, premiums would skyrocket in order to pay for all the minor repairs, the cost of completing and transferring paperwork, adjusting claims, issuing payments, paying executives, and making a profit. Some consumers may reduce costs by making minor repairs on a "DIY" basis or accepting wear and tear as one of the realities of owning a car. By absorbing routine costs themselves, *consumers avoid the evils of first dollar coverage.* The higher the deductible, the lower the insurance premium and wise consumers save a lot of money by choosing high deductible insurance. If their car is old, they may even skip collision insurance altogether, putting their premium dollars into liability insurance where the risk of large, catastrophic claims is much greater.

First Dollar Health Insurance Is Bad Insurance

Buying health insurance that covers the expected, normal, noncatastrophic costs of health care is bad insurance. When routine medical expenses are paid by insurance instead of directly by consumers, total costs rise. Not only must the insurance company perform all of its functions at a profit, physicians must spend more time managing an increasing number of office workers, filling out paperwork, and substantiating claims for reimbursement. That time could be spent more productively providing patient *care*. That's why a $25 visit to a "cash and carry" doctor may cost $70 in offices reimbursed by insurance.

How Did We Ever Get into This Situation?

Go back a century or more and you'll discover that hospitals were mostly for the indigent. At a time when technology was no better in hospitals than in homes, patients too ill to travel to the doctor's office would receive a house call from a physician who would advise the family on the patient's condition. The care provided by family members (as well as the food!) was usually better in homes than in hospitals. For most consumers, the cost of health care was primarily the physician's fee and a few medicines blended at the local apothecary. When the poor had no families or inadequate homes, care was offered by charity hospitals operated by religious or governmental entities.

As technology improved, especially for surgery and specialized procedures, hospitals became better positioned to care for patients than homes. Whereas families had previously incurred only the small cost of physician's fees (in rural areas, physicians were sometimes paid with farm produce), institutional care added a comparatively large expense. As a result, hospitals often encountered patients who could not pay their bills.

To survive, in the early 1930s hospitals organized the not-for-profit Blue Cross Association. In exchange for a small monthly premium of approximately 75 cents per month deducted from employees' paychecks or paid by employers (whose owners were often members of the hospital board), Blue Cross covered the nearly catastrophic cost of a hospital stay for the average worker. Such was "good insurance" in that a small fee collected from many people made funds available for large, infrequent expenditures. Blue Cross worked so well that ten years later, physicians organized a similar plan called Blue Shield to pay for medical services. Originally for "major medical" (surgery or unusually high expenses) coverage was extended over time to all services, becoming "minor medical" as well. Thus, the evils of first dollar coverage were born.

These early insurance programs grew rapidly, emulated by aggressive for-profit insurance carriers that were not limited to the geographic boundaries of Blue Cross/Blue Shield plans. Over time, some BC/BS plans also shifted to "for profit" status to compete with private insurance companies benefiting from growth opportunities in the health care insurance business. Today, most insurance companies are massive, nationwide bureaucracies seeking to maximize profits by insuring as much of health care as possible.

Now that consumers are accustomed to insurance paying for nearly every health care expense and allowing employers, the government and other third parties to control health care decisions, the natural inclination is to let those parties "fix" the system. In Texas there is a term for making improvements to a process that ought not to exist at all. It's called "paving the cow path and polishing the turds." Third-party indirect costs mean the current system is inherently inefficient; any improvements will produce nominal results at best.

Reducing the Evils of First Dollar Coverage

Do consumers want to start paying their own health care costs again?

Of course not, but with higher deductibles, higher co-pays, and higher employee contributions to health insurance premiums, consumers are paying more of their health care costs whether they want to or not. The alternative may be no benefits (or possibly no job) at all.

Workers in employer-sponsored health plans in 2003 paid 48 percent more out of their own pockets for health care than they did three years earlier, according to a study by the Kaiser Family Foundation and the Health Research and Educational Trust. Instead of the current 23 percent employees pay, nearly 80 percent of large employers plan on raising the amount of employee contributions. Some firms require that employees pay 50 percent of the *rise* in insurance premiums, but others now split the *total* premium fifty-fifty.

Health insurance premiums rose 13.9 percent in 2003, outpacing the 11 percent rise in spending for hospitals and doctors, and far ahead of the 2.4 percent increase in manufacturers' prices, according to the Kaiser study. For small employers with fewer than 300 workers, the increase was 15.6 percent. Employers have three alternatives to asking employees to pay a higher proportion of health insurance: eliminate benefits altogether, reduce the number of employees, or go out of business. When faced with these choices, it's easy to understand why employees grudgingly accept higher deductions from their paychecks for health insurance. When consumers become equal pay-ers of health insurance premiums in consumer driven health care, their attention is focused on rising costs and the solutions they can adopt to reverse the trend.

Shifting a greater share of premiums to employees has plenty of opposition. Voters in the state of California recently considered a "pay or play" law requiring larger firms not only to provide private health insurance for all employees, but also "pay" for 80 percent of the premiums. Employers who choose not to provide coverage are forced to "play" by contributing to a state fund for the purchase of private insurance. California already faces fiscal crisis as rising taxes and labor costs push jobs to other Western states. Although the leg-islation would have assured private health insurance for a large per-centage of Californians, the addition of $7 billion in new taxes could also have spelled economic disaster. Consumers don't like increasing their proportion of insurance premiums, but the alternative may be no job at all.

In addition to shifting premiums to consumers, the evils of first dollar coverage may be reduced by increasing co-pay amounts. Typi-cal insurance plans require co-pays of $25 to $40 per doctor's visit or prescription. When employers apply the co-pay principle to hospital stays, adding deductibles of $100 to $250 per stay, the effect is very similar to auto insurance policies. The ultimate co-pay is 100 percent for every health care purchase below some maximum amount each year, typically $1,000 per individual or $2,000 per family. Such "high deductible" policies accompanied by a Health Savings Account over-come the bad decisions likely to occur when "someone else" pays, and force consumers to budget for normal, expected health care costs just as they do for food, clothing, housing and other necessities.

The result? Consumers will become as proficient in purchasing health care as they are for all other consumer goods and services, ask-ing doctors and hospitals the price of their services and comparing competitive offerings. They will ask themselves, "Is this trip to the doctor really necessary?" and if not, consider alternative or over-the-counter remedies. They may also watch their weight, quit smoking, and avoid activities likely to result in accident or illness. Eliminating first dollar coverage with high deductible policies provides a major economic incentive for the most important strategy for reducing health care costs—*maintaining better health.*

> *Solution for America's "Two Trillion Dollar Crisis": Change existing health insurance policies to high deductible policies eliminating first dollar coverage and putting consumers back in charge of their routine health care expenditures.*

Why Health Savings Accounts May Shake the Foundations of the Health Care System

Health Savings Accounts (HSAs) were created as part of the Medicare Prescription Drug, Modernization and Improvement Act, enacted on December 8, 2003. The easiest way to understand an HSA is to describe it as a "health IRA" that combines the strengths of both traditional and Roth IRAs. In a traditional IRA, contributions are tax-deductible and balances grow tax-deferred, but taxes are paid on both principal and earnings when withdrawn. Roth IRA contributions are made with after-tax dollars, but principal and earnings are not normally taxed when withdrawn. An HSA offers the best of both worlds in that contributions are tax deductible when made, balances grow tax-deferred and principal and earnings are not taxed when withdrawn. The caveat is that consumers can only open their HSA treasure chests to pay for health care, including physician and prescription co-pays, and other uninsured expenditures including dental, orthodontics, chiropractic, laser eye surgery, contact lenses, and some over-the-counter remedies—not only for HSA owners, but also for their spouses and dependents. (For a list of what can be paid with an HSA, see Exhibit 7.5.)

An HSA is available *only* to people in high deductible health plans who are not covered by other health insurance, who are not enrolled in Medicare, and who cannot be claimed as a dependent on someone else's tax return (meaning children cannot establish their own HSAs). Qualifying health plans include HMOs, PPOs, and indemnity plans that have a minimum deductible of $1,000 (individual) or $2,000 (family), with annual out-of-pocket expenditures (including deductibles and co-pays) not exceeding $5,000 (individual) or $10,000 (family). All amounts are indexed for inflation. While high deductible health plans can provide first dollar coverage for preventive care and require higher out-of-pocket expenditures for nonnetwork services, other first dollar benefits such as Medicare, Tricare, Flexible Spending Accounts and Health Reimbursement Accounts render the policy ineligible for an HSA. Likewise, if state or local laws require any first dollar coverage to be written into a policy, the policy cannot be considered high deductible for HSA purposes after 2006. Preventive care services that do not count towards the deductible include annual physicals, screening services such as mammograms, prenatal care, immunizations, tobacco cessation, and obesity weight loss programs.

HSAs generally can't reimburse beneficiaries' health insurance premiums on a tax-favored basis, but they can pay for qualified long-term care insurance premiums, COBRA continuation coverage premiums, and health insurance premiums paid while receiving state or federal unemployment benefits. HSA distributions used for nonmedical purposes are taxed the same as early distributions from IRAs or 401(k) plans and are subject to a 10 percent penalty, but the penalty does not apply if the HSA beneficiary is disabled or age 65. When an account beneficiary dies, the HSA can pass to his or her surviving spouse on a tax-free basis. (As of publication, most states have yet to determine whether contributions are also deductible from state income taxes.)

HSAs replace the well-intentioned, but fatally-flawed MSA and FSA accounts (described in Exhibit 7.1) that allowed consumers to pay part of their uninsured medical bills with before-tax dollars. Unlike HSAs, these "use it or lose it" programs required consumers to estimate their medical bills for the coming year, deduct that amount from their paychecks, and then submit covered expenses for reimbursement. The fatal flaw was that if consumers didn't spend the total amount they estimated the year before, they lost it forever. Instead of providing a mechanism for consumers to save for health care expenses, MSAs/FSAs create an incentive to spend it all, often just prior to year-end.

HSAs provide additional advantages over MSAs and FSAs. Whereas MSAs/FSAs involve a costly and time-consuming claims reimbursement process, HSAs provide a checkbook or debit card to facilitate transactions at point of purchase. Consumers track their own expenditures. Of course, the onus falls on consumers to also know what constitutes "eligible expenditures" and to save all receipts should they ever be audited.

Total contributions from all sources to an individual's HSA currently cannot exceed the lesser of the attached high deductible health plan's annual deductible of $2,600 ($5,150 for family coverage). Unlike MSAs/FSAs and HRAs, HSA limits are inflation-adjusted and increased by $500 for eligible individuals who are at least 50 years old, but not yet eligible for Medicare. This "catch-up" increases annually in $100 increments until it reaches $1,000 in 2009, but is not subject to inflation adjustments.

Unlike previous plans, HSAs are completely portable, belonging to an employee even after he or she leaves a job or the attached high deductible insurance policy terminates. There are no income limits on who may contribute to an HSA and individuals can make tax-deductible contributions even if they do not itemize deductions on their federal income tax returns. Employers can make tax-favored contributions to HSAs for all employees, regardless of income, although employees can fund their own HSA if their employer does not. In fact, contributions can be made by others (including family members) on behalf of an account holder and still be deducted by the account holder.

People who invest regularly in an HSA during their working years and are careful about their health expenditures could have hundreds of thousands of dollars available for hospitals, doctor visits, pharmaceuticals, or any other healthcare related purpose when they retire. Because HSAs use before-tax money for medical expenses, consumers who try to stay healthy should have money available in their retirement years to relieve worries that plague today's seniors including prescription drug coverage (generally not covered by Medicare) or living longer than they can afford, especially should the projected 2019 bankruptcy of Medicare occur. Remember, the majority of lifetime medical expenses occur later in life, so for many people, investment income from their HSAs could become large enough to pay uninsured, routine health costs for the rest of their lives. This may be difficult if contributions receive only checking account yields, but as competition increases, higher-yield investment options will become more widely available.

Thanks to HSAs, for the first time in decades consumers have an economic incentive to be healthy. Under most current employer-funded insurance plans, unhealthy people pay the same premiums as healthy people, providing little economic incentive to eat well, exercise, and live carefully. The current system is unfair to people who make good choices because they end up subsidizing those who do not. With an HSA, the economic benefits of being healthy accrue to people who are healthy. When people have ownership of their own healthcare expenditures, they avoid going to doctors unless really necessary, they compare prices, and they patronize innovative "Southwest Airlines style" providers or specialty hospitals. Because an HSA must be accompanied by a high deducible health insurance policy, it helps eliminate the evils of first dollar coverage while encouraging wellness. As a catalyst to better health and more efficient health care delivery, the HSA will bring forth consumer driven health care and dramatically reduce America's "Two Trillion Dollar Crisis."

The Big Threats to Health Savings Accounts

There are three significant threats to HSAs. One is that Congress will be pressured to lower the required deductible for the attached health insurance policy, mandate how the accounts are administered (perhaps even requiring that expenses be submitted to a government agency for approval), or limit the amount that can be withdrawn for certain services (regardless of the actual price of the service). Such would embed a third-party payer and defeat the goal of eliminating the evils of first dollar coverage.

Second is that many consumers won't understand it, won't budget for it, and that only the wisest and most financially competent consumers will take advantage of it. Consumers who continue to buy comprehensive insurance may fear they are not "automatically" taken care of in all contingencies. If they are accustomed to paying only $20 every time they see a doctor or fill a prescription, they may feel like they have no insurance at all (despite having full catastrophic coverage). Such prevailing attitudes could defeat the goal of rewarding those who save for their own health care. This barrier is overcome by demonstrating to consumers that first dollar coverage is a poor value. In some cases, employers may also choose to partially fund HSAs as they currently do 401(k)s. Because 80 percent of all people in traditional first-dollar health plans never spend enough to cover their deductibles, the money spent on low deductible insurance is lost. With HSAs, instead of giving the difference to an insurance company, it goes into a personal account that reduces taxable income, grows tax-deferred, and is available tax-free whenever it is needed for routine medical expenses. Rather than worry about not being taken care of, consumers should feel empowered in making their own health care decisions—today and in the future.

Third is that the ultimate success of HSAs will be determined by how well they are marketed. While insurance companies could certainly benefit from more predictable risk and greater cost control in high deductible policies, more policyholders due to greater affordability (as well as generally younger and healthier consumers who don't require first dollar coverage), a positive float on deposits, and less paperwork processing, many may be hesitant to market a service that potentially decreases premium revenues, invested reserves, processing fees, and general power over health care. Although most large health insurers currently provide HSAs, many have yet to recommend or advertise them. Instead, their attitude is "wait and see." The push will have to come from employers who are struggling to remain profitable and who realize the cost savings of high deductible policies are essential for retaining their health care benefit plans.

The best opportunity to protect against these threats is that people like you understand the role an HSA can play in your financial future and why the HSA is a key component in consumer driven health care. Awareness and knowledge are the weapons of choice in the war on health care costs and, hopefully, this book contributes to both.

Solving the Uninsured Problem

A critically important issue facing the nation is what to do about the 45 million Americans who have no health insurance. About ten million of these uninsured are between the ages of 25 and 34. These young adults really should have only one type of health insurance—high deductible for "major medical" or catastrophic illness. Young people have some medical expenses, but generally far fewer than older adults. Yet, many young adults still pay high premiums to cover the cost of routine, expected medical care.

It's not unusual for young people in good health to pay less than $100 a month for a high deductible policy compared to $250 to $500 for traditional first dollar coverage. If this difference were invested in an HSA, they could accumulate a large enough nest egg by middle age or retirement to pay most of their nonreimbursed medical care directly from their HSA. Even if young people do face major medical bills, with a high deductible policy paying 80 to 100 percent after the deductible is met, they probably have better coverage of those bills than with conventional policies with co-insurance requirements of 20 to 50 percent.

An HSA is especially valuable to younger consumers in raising awareness of health care prices, buying from efficient providers, and learning to make healthy choices. It may take a few years for these lessons to be diffused widely, but they help reduce the number of uninsured by making low cost health insurance available for when catastrophic problems occur—the ones that cause the greatest collections problems. Hospitals should love the fact that the low premiums of high deductible policies reduce the large number of uninsured consumers with uncollectible bills that burden their balance sheets. And lower overall health care costs from more efficient health care providers should provide greater options for those on Medicare or Medicaid.

HSAs will create motivation to improve the efficiency of the health care system and release funds from employer and government payers to do other important things. One possibility could be to use some of the savings generated to assist states with the desperate situation facing their Medicaid programs. Another possibility could be the creation of a program, administered by individual states, that provides catastrophic health insurance for low income families unable to cope with the costs of treating long-term illnesses. Although beyond the scope of this book, consumer driven health care will be the catalyst for many such reforms.

Are You All Ready for This?

The HSA is a new weapon available to fight the evils of first dollar coverage. As the popular song often played at sporting events asks, "Are you all ready for this?" understanding why first dollar coverage is bad insurance is only the beginning—you must also demand your employer offer high deductible insurance plans. If your employer currently offers HSAs, it may need to change its annual benefits enrollment materials and other communications to convince employees and their families (and in some cases, labor unions) to start budgeting for routine health care the same way they do for food, clothing, rent, and other necessities.

Next, you have to select the right HSA plan. Most employers will assume leadership in that decision, but if you're not satisfied with your employer's choices, you will have to make your own search and decision. And you will have to decide which investment option to place your funds. If the only option is an FDIC-insured deposit account, the yield will be so low you won't see much growth in unspent funds. The best programs should combine checking account convenience (usually low yield) with a "sweep" to higher yielding options (such as money market or mutual funds) when balances reach a specified amount. Most companies are just getting started with attractive, competitive programs so it may take several years for marketing and sales programs to evolve into in the most competitive products.

Why will the HSA reform health care? Because an HSA puts consumers in the driver's seat, back to the roots of health care more than a half-century ago. As health care evolves from a third-party payer system to consumer driven health care, expect consumers to buy health care with the same proficiency with which they buy groceries.

Exhibit 7.1   Features of Some Types of Health Accounts Offered By Employers

	Health FSAs[1]	HRAs[2]	HSAs[3]
Coordinate with other plan?	No	No. However, it is often integrated with a high deductible plan.	Yes. In order to contribute to a HSA, an individual must participate in a "high-deductible health plan"[4]
Allow employer contributions?	Yes	Yes	Yes
Allow employee contributions?	Yes	No	Yes
Pre-tax employee contributions permitted?	Yes	No	Yes
Prescribed maximum contributions?	None	None	Yes. The lesser of high deductible plan deductible or $2,600 ($5,150 family), plus "catch-up" contributions.[5]
Carry over of unused amounts to next year?	No	Yes	Yes
"Use it or lose it" rule apply?	Yes	No	No
Rollovers permitted?	No	No	Yes, from other HSAs and from MSAs
Must accounts be "funded" (i.e., held outside employer general assets)	No	No	Yes

1. A health flexible spending account ("Health FSA") is self-insured medical reimbursement program established under Code section 105. This type of account is often used in conjunction with a Code section 125 cafeteria plan.

2. A health reimbursement arrangement ("HRA") was recognized by the Internal Revenue Service in Revenue Ruling 2002–41 and Notice 2002–45.

3. The health savings account ("HSA") was established, effective January 1, 2004, as part of the Medicare Prescription Drug, Improvement, and Modernization Act of 2003. This account can be established by an employer on behalf of an employee or by the employee him/herself if the other conditions are met.

4. A "high deductible health plan" is a medical plan which has annual deductibles of at least $1,000 for individual coverage and $2,000 for family coverage and which limits out-of-pocket expenses for participants to not more than $5,000 for individual coverage or $10,000 for family coverage. For managed care plans, these amounts apply to the in-network benefits and not the out-of-network portion of the plan. A plan which offers first dollar "preventive care" benefits may still be considered a high deductible health plan if it meets the other requirements.

Participants who turn 55 have an opportunity to make "catch-up" contributions. The maximum catch-up contributions are $500 for 2004, $600 for 2005, $700 for 2006, $800 for 2007, $900 for $2008, and $1,000 for 2009 and thereafter. The $1,000 amount will be indexed.

Some HSA/HRA/FSA combinations are permitted.

Attributes of traditional health plans

```
┌─────────────────────┐    ┌─────────────────────┐    ┌─────────────────────┐
│ Health insurance    │    │ Policy outlines     │    │ Policy covers both  │
│ premium is paid by  │───▶│ authorized services,│───▶│ routine and         │
│ employer,           │    │ eligible providers, │    │ catastrophic        │
│ employee, or both.  │    │ and standard pricing.│   │ expenditures.       │
└─────────────────────┘    └─────────────────────┘    └─────────────────────┘

┌─────────────────────┐    ┌─────────────────────┐    ┌─────────────────────┐
│                     │    │ Patient covers co-  │    │ Policy covers both  │
│ Expenditures are    │    │ pays, deductibles,  │    │ routine and         │
│ subject to 20 to    │◀───│ and other out-of-   │◀───│ catastrophic        │
│ 50% co-insurance.   │    │ pocket expenses with│    │ expenditures.       │
│                     │    │ after-tax dollars.  │    │                     │
└─────────────────────┘    └─────────────────────┘    └─────────────────────┘
```

Non-medical and uncovered services including over-the-counter medications and supplies, chiropractic, dental, and vision care are paid with after-tax dollars.

Exhibit 7.2   Attributes of Traditional Health Plans

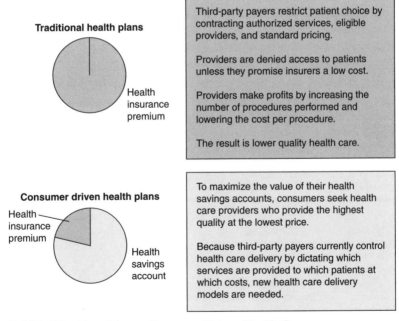

Traditional health plans

Health insurance premium

Third-party payers restrict patient choice by contracting authorized services, eligible providers, and standard pricing.

Providers are denied access to patients unless they promise insurers a low cost.

Providers make profits by increasing the number of procedures performed and lowering the cost per procedure.

The result is lower quality health care.

Consumer driven health plans

Health insurance premium

Health savings account

To maximize the value of their health savings accounts, consumers seek health care providers who provide the highest quality at the lowest price.

Because third-party payers currently control health care delivery by dictating which services are provided to which patients at which costs, new health care delivery models are needed.

Exhibit 7.3   Transition to Consumer Driven Health Care

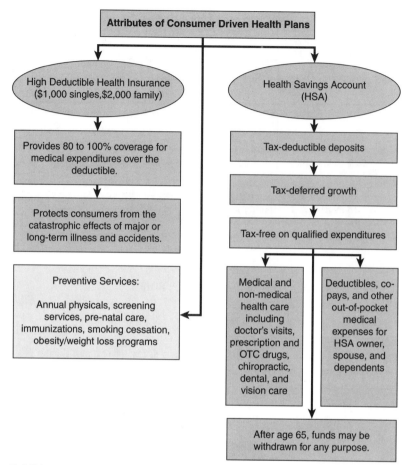

Exhibit 7.4

Exhibit 7.5   What expenses can be paid by a Health Savings Account?

Eligible medical expenses are defined as those expenses paid for care as described in Section 213(d) of the Internal Revenue Code. Additionally, the IRS has allowed some over-the-counter drugs to qualify as eligible medical expenses (*Revenue Ruling 2003–102, 2003–38 I.R.B. 559*).

Eligible Medical Expenses

Abdominal supports
Abortion
Acupuncture
Air conditioner (when necessary for relief from difficulty in breathing)
Alcoholism treatment
Ambulance
Anesthetist
Arch supports
Artificial limbs
Autoette (when used for relief of sickness/disability)
Birth Control Pills (by prescription)
Blood Tests
Blood transfusions
Braces
Cardiographs
Chiropractor
Christian Science Practitioner
Contact Lenses
Contraceptive devices (by prescription)
Convalescent home (for medical treatment only)
Crutches
Dental Treatment
Dental x-rays
Dentures
Dermatologist
Diagnostic fees
Diathermy
Drug addiction therapy

Drugs (prescription)
Elastic hosiery (prescription)
Eyeglasses
Fees paid to health institute prescribed by a doctor
FICA and FUTA tax paid for medical care service
Fluoridation unit
Guide dog
Gum treatment
Gynecologist
Healing services
Hearing aids and batteries
Hospital bills
Hydrotherapy
Insulin treatment
Lab tests
Lead paint removal
Legal fees
Lodging (away from home for outpatient care)
Metabolism tests
Neurologist
Nursing (including board and meals)
Obstetrician
Operating room costs
Ophthalmologist
Optician
Optometrist
Oral surgery
Organ transplant (including donor's expenses)
Orthopedic shoes
Orthopedist

Osteopath
Oxygen and oxygen equipment
Pediatrician
Physician
Physiotherapist
Podiatrist
Postnatal treatments
Practical nurse for medical services
Prenatal care
Prescription medicines
Psychiatrist
Psychoanalyst
Psychologist
Psychotherapy
Radium Therapy
Registered nurse
Special school costs for the handicapped
Spinal fluid test
Splints
Sterilization
Surgeon
Telephone or TV equipment to assist the hard-of-hearing
Therapy equipment
Transportation expenses (relative to health care)
Ultra-violet ray treatment
Vaccines
Vasectomy
Vitamins (if prescribed)
Wheelchair
X-rays

(continued)

Exhibit 7.5   What expenses can be paid by a Health Savings Account? (*continued*)

Eligible Over-the-Counter Drugs

Antacids
Allergy Medications
Pain Relievers
Cold medicine
Anti-diarrhea medicine
Cough drops and throat
   lozenges

Sinus medications and nasal
   sprays
Nicotine medications and
   nasal sprays
Pedialyte
First aid creams
Calamine lotion

Wart removal medication
Antibiotic ointments
Suppositories and creams
   for hemorrhoids
Sleep aids
Motion sickness pills

Ineligible Medical Expenses

Advancement payment for
   services to be rendered
   next year
Athletic club membership
Automobile insurance
   premium allocable to
   medical coverage
Boarding school fees
Bottled water
Commuting expenses of a
   disabled person
Cosmetic surgery and
   procedures
Cosmetics, hygiene products
   and similar items

Funeral, cremation, or
   burial expenses
Health programs offered by
   resort hotels, health clubs,
   and gyms
Illegal operations and
   treatments
Illegally procured drugs
Maternity clothes
Non-prescription
   medication
Premiums for life insurance,
   income protection,
   disability, loss of limbs,
   sight or similar benefits

Scientology counseling
Social activities
Special foods and beverages
Specially designed car for
   the handicapped other
   than an autoette or special
   equipment
Stop-smoking programs
Swimming pool
Travel for general health
   improvement
Tuition and travel expenses
   a problem child to a
   particular school
Weight loss programs

Ineligible Over-the-Counter Drugs

Toiletries (including
   toothpaste)
Acne treatments
Lip balm
Cosmetics (including face
   cream and moisturizer)

Suntan lotion
Medicated shampoos and
   soaps
Vitamins (daily)
Fiber supplements

Dietary supplements
Weight loss drugs for
   general well-being
Herbs

Important Notice: This list is not to be construed as tax advice, but rather, to illustrate the value of an HSA to consumers. For more detailed information, please refer to IRS Publication 502 or contact a tax professional.

CHAPTER 8

More Health Care Is Not the Answer

"Nothing is more terrible than activity without insight."
—Thomas Carlyle

Imagine you're a young physician standing on the bank of a river. Suddenly, you hear the screams of someone drowning nearby so you jump into the river, pull the victim out, and resuscitate him. Breathing a sigh of relief that your medical training, loyalty to your Hippocratic oath, and your desire to help people in distress have saved a human life, you glance back to the river only to see two more people drowning. As you attempt to rescue them, you hear the cries of even more drowning people—first dozens, then hundreds, and finally thousands! You frantically do your best to save as many as you can, but the task is too great. Despite your best efforts, many drown, leaving you to wonder, "Why are all these people in the river?" Yet it's someone else's job to tell people that if they swim in this river, they are likely to drown. Millions of people jumping of their own volition into the "river of bad health" are a poignant symbol of what's happening in the American health care system.

Will More Medicine Cause Better Health?

Health care dollars in the United States are focused on "sickness care," as described in Chapter 1, and funded by a higher proportion of GDP than any other country in the world. Comparatively little is spent on preventive measures and public health that might keep all those drowning people out of the river. Spending more money on more doctors pulling more people out of rivers doesn't do much to reduce the flood of unhealthy lifestyles that consumers create for themselves, leading to poor health and shortened lives.

Average life expectancy in the United States increased by 30 years during the twentieth century, yet only five years of that increase was due to "pulling people out of the river," commonly called "curative medicine," delivered mostly by "institutional" health care. Exhibit 8.1 illustrates the relationship between longevity or good health and the role of curative medicine in extending life. Healthy people generally shouldn't require the services of institutional health care until disease sets in (usually toward the end of their lives). Nevertheless, consumers frequently adopt lifestyles that cause poor health early in life, forfeiting the opportunity to experience healthy living (as well as overall quality of life), increased longevity and low health care costs. That's what happens when a nation focuses its resources on "sickness" care instead of "health" care.

Despite the average 25 years of longevity made possible by advances in public health and disease prevention over the last century, current yearly state and federal spending average only $1.21 per person on preventive care compared to $1,390 for medical treatment of disease. Because the demand for institutional health care is so great and billions of dollars are made each year by pharmaceutical and medical device manufacturers, hospitals, insurance companies, physicians and others "rescuing" the drowning masses, there is little incentive for those in the "business" of health care to shift spending

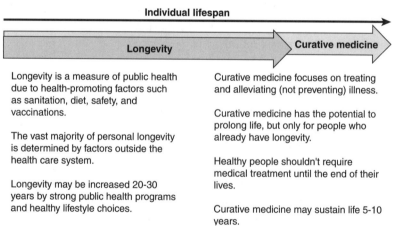

Individual lifespan

Longevity   Curative medicine

Longevity is a measure of public health due to health-promoting factors such as sanitation, diet, safety, and vaccinations.

The vast majority of personal longevity is determined by factors outside the health care system.

Longevity may be increased 20-30 years by strong public health programs and healthy lifestyle choices.

Curative medicine focuses on treating and alleviating (not preventing) illness.

Curative medicine has the potential to prolong life, but only for people who already have longevity.

Healthy people shouldn't require medical treatment until the end of their lives.

Curative medicine may sustain life 5-10 years.

Exhibit 8.1   Longevity vs. Institutional Medicine: Roger Blackwell Associates, 2004

away from curative medicine and invest in prevention. For $50,000 or more, a surgeon may perform cardio-bypass surgery, and with proper rehab and lifestyle changes, extend the life of a patient five to ten years. Or, for a few pennies, a child can be taught proper diet and exercise, and 50 or 60 years from now, completely avoid heart disease. The former provides immediate revenue impacting someone's bottom line; the latter is an immediate expense that somehow has to be paid. As a result, decisions regarding preventive medicine are almost always made as a matter of public policy by individuals outside the health care system.

In Chapter 3 you read that Singapore's public health emphasis achieves greater longevity than the United States, at less than one-third the cost. Some nations focus more on prevention as a matter of necessity. In the United Kingdom, for instance, a system of socialized medicine results in rationing of medical procedures. If a public policy decision is made that only 2,000 kidney transplants will be paid for in a given year yet there are 5,000 people on waiting lists, limited funds are better spent promoting ways to keep kidneys healthy so fewer transplants are required. In the United States, where unlimited funds are available for kidney transplants (paid by "someone else") and the only limitation is the availability of donor kidneys, the prevention of kidney disease ends up spread across many medical disciplines without any specific focus. In modern societies, many benefits of disease prevention represent past accomplishments now taken for granted. One has only to look at developing countries to see how the miracle of preventive medicine can change the health of an entire population in a relatively short period of time, as the following example illustrates.

In Malawi, GI dysentery historically was the leading cause of sickness and death, primarily because the water there frequently becomes contaminated by animal and human waste. According to Dr. Walter Hull, an American missionary physician, preventive medicine has eliminated the problem for many. The "miracle cure" was not a breakthrough drug, but rather, the work of volunteers from a Marion, Illinois church who dug about 1,300 wells, sparing seven percent of Malawi's population from cholera and other diseases associated with contaminated water (www.marionmedical.org).

Preventive health care goes much deeper than deep wells, of course, because the United States, for the most part, has a clean and generally safe infrastructure. For the United States, preventive medicine means moving from public health to personal health—the choices people make and the ways people live.

Testing the Theory that More Money Means Better Health

Variations in longevity and health care costs in the United States are sometimes as great between states as between the United States and other countries, because the United States does not have a truly "national" health care system. Death rates are significantly higher in the South, for example, than in the Rocky Mountain region, as Exhibit 8.2 shows. While average life expectancy in the United States is 74.4 years for men and 79.8 years for women, Utah exceeds the national average by about three years and Mississippi falls short by about three years. To understand why health is determined by structural variables (education, culture, lifestyles, and health care availability) rather than health care expenditures, study the differences in health outcomes in states at opposite ends of the spectrum—Utah and Mississippi.

Utah: More for Less

Settled by Brigham Young in 1847 and inhabited by thousands of pioneers who traveled across the Great Plains until about 1890, the state of Utah currently has a population of 2.3 million, of whom 70 to 75 percent identify with the Church of Jesus Christ of Latter-day Saints (LDS), also known as Mormons. A number of demographic and sociological studies document that a high proportion of Utah residents follow the LDS moral and dietary rules which include pursuit of higher education, sexual abstinence outside of marriage, missionary and community service, and total avoidance of alcohol, tobacco, coffee and illegal drugs. Although other religious groups, including Seventh-day Adventists, have similar codes of conduct, no other group dominates a single geographical area, making the LDS unique in the availability of government statistics.

Utah has the lowest adult and teenage smoking rates in the country (12.1 percent), and a risk for heart disease 20 percent below the national average. It also has the lowest number of cancer cases, the

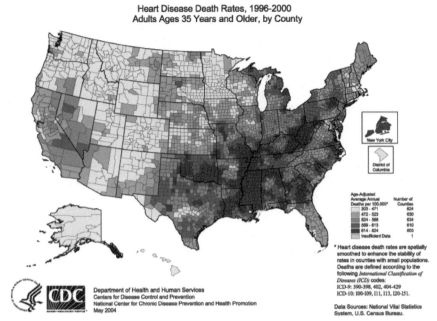

Heart Disease Death Rates, 1996-2000
Adults Ages 35 Years and Older, by County

Exhibit 8.2   Heart Disease Death Rates, West Virginia University and Centers for Disease Control and Prevention, 2004. Darkest areas represent counties with the greatest average annual deaths from heart disease (per 100,000)

lowest number of days missed from work due to illness, the fourth lowest infant mortality rate, the lowest teen pregnancy rate, the lowest abortion rate, the fewest number of children born to unwed mothers, the fewest one-parent families, the lowest child poverty rate, and it produces more scientists per capita than any other state.

Utah's public education system ranks seventh in the nation for overall quality, second in the percentage of high school graduates, and first for number of advanced placement (AP) tests passed, despite ranking 49th for total educational expenditures per pupil. Provo, home of Brigham Young University, has been rated by *Self* magazine (2000) as the "healthiest city in the country for women." In fact, LDS women are more likely than either Catholic or Protestant women to be college graduates and 23 percent of LDS women are employed in professional occupations, second only to Jewish women (www.adherents.com).

Utah ranks first in the number of homes with personal computers (65 percent), first in individual charitable giving, and has crime rates significantly below national averages. Utah also has a highly structured establishment for institutional medicine dominated by Intermountain Health Care with costs 28 percent below the national average, as you read about in Chapter 5.

In a study by *Demographic Research* ("Life Expectancy among LDS and Non-LDS in Utah," Merrill, Roy M., March 12, 2004), the life expectancy of LDS members in Utah was 77.3 for men and 82.2 for women versus 70.0 and 76.4 for non-LDS. While abstinence from tobacco explains some of the higher life expectancy in LDS, the study concludes it accounts for only 1.5 of the 7.3-year difference for men and only 1.2 of the 5.8-year difference for women. Rather, higher life expectancy among Mormons is explained by better physical health, healthier lifestyle behaviors, better social support, and religious faith.

By combining a culture that promotes health and wellness with a health care delivery system focused on providing high quality care at affordable prices, Utah has achieved the greatest longevity in the United States yet the amount spent on personal health care expenditures is well below the national average.

Mississippi: Less for More

Way down South in the land of "Rock and Roll" and the "Delta Blues," where it is often as hot as it is humid, is the state of Mississippi. Cotton, timber, poultry, and catfish are the major agricultural products of this flat, largely rural home to some of the most fertile soil on earth, which also has a rising tourism industry due to Native American and riverboat casinos. Although no single religious group represents a majority of Mississippians, the state's religious affiliations consist largely of Protestant denominations, most notably Baptist and Methodist. Until 1940, African-Americans made up the majority of Mississippi's population, and today Mississippi has the largest proportion of African-Americans of any state, making up about 40 percent of the state's 2.8 million total population. Ninety-eight percent of Mississippians were born in the state (highest in the United States) and the white population is among the most homogenous in the nation consisting of individuals from British, Irish, and Northern European ancestry (www.mississippistatecenter.com).

Mississippi has a high poverty rate of 22.8 percent, and one out of every three children in Mississippi lives in poverty. A greater percentage of children than in the nation as a whole are born out of wedlock (nearly half the children born in Mississippi) and live in one-parent families. The rate of births to teens, at 76 per 1,000, is 41 percent higher than the national average. In fact, 22 percent of all live births in Mississippi are to teenage mothers, and approximately 35 percent of teen mothers with one baby will have a second baby during their teenage years. Mississippi has the highest percentage of low birth-weight babies; the highest infant mortality and child death rates; and the highest rate of teen deaths by accident, homicide, and suicide. Overall, Mississippi ranks 49th on a composite rating of 10 selected measures of child well-being (Urban Institute, 1998). According to the CDC, Mississippi (along with Georgia and South Carolina) also is among the most sexually promiscuous populations with the consequent highest adult rates of gonorrhea, syphilis, and other sexually transmitted diseases.

Mississippi has the lowest adult literacy rate at 64 percent (national average is 97 percent), ranks 46th for high school graduates and has the lowest rate of Internet usage in the United States (23 percent). In 2004, Mississippi's unemployment rate was higher than the national average with individual counties ranging from 18 (Jefferson) to 2.3 percent (Hancock). Along with four other southern states, Mississippi has a high percentage of its residents incarcerated, and although Mississippi is largely rural, major cities in the region such as Jackson, Memphis, and New Orleans lead the nation in violent crime.

How do these factors translate to personal health and health care expenditures? Three risk behaviors in particular—tobacco use, lack of physical activity, and poor nutrition—are major contributors to cardiovascular disease and cancer, the nation's leading killers. They also elevate the life threatening complications of diabetes.

According to the Mississippi State Department of Health, Mississippi has the highest death rate from cardiovascular disease (CVD) in the nation, with one Mississippian dying of heart disease every 45 minutes, 29 percent higher than the United States in 2002. CVD is the leading cause of death in Mississippi, accounting for 41 percent of all deaths in the state—more than all types of cancer, traffic accidents, suicides, and AIDS combined. The economic impact of CVD on the Mississippi health care system was estimated at $3.7 billion in 2001 and will continue to grow with the advancing age of the population.

The second leading cause of death in Mississippi is cancer, accounting for 21 percent of all deaths in 2001. Of all states, Mississippi had the third highest rate of cancer in 1999, including the third highest rate of death due to lung cancer. Mississippi's adult smoking rate, at 33.2 percent, is significantly higher than the national average of 25.9 percent (CDC Morbidity and Mortality Weekly Report, January 9, 2004). In Africa, where smoking is not affordable for most people, there is almost *no* lung cancer.

Diabetes, while not tracked as a direct cause of death, afflicts 270,000 Mississippians or 9.3 percent of the population. More than 1,700 Mississippians suffer significant diabetes-related complications each year, including blindness and amputations. In 1997, the estimated cost of diabetes in Mississippi was about $1.7 billion and has risen since then.

Although Mississippi does not have a statewide health care delivery system like Utah's Intermountain Health Care, Mississippians are equally covered by health insurance (86.9 percent) as Utahns (86.0 percent). This fact is significant in that the difference in personal health between the states cannot be attributed to access to curative medicine. Rather, the primary causes of chronic disease are determined by personal choices regarding smoking, diet, and regular physical activity. As you can observe in Table 8.3, the incidence of these factors is higher in Mississippi.

The result of unhealthy lifestyles in Mississippi is average personal health care expenditures that are 48 percent higher than the rest of the nation. While a large part of this difference is attributed to the fact there is simply more disease to treat, the indirect costs of health care are also much higher.

Although Mississippi has a smaller percentage of uninsured residents than Utah, Mississippi does have a significantly higher rate of individuals covered by government programs such as Medicaid and Medicare as opposed to private insurance. According to the Mississippi Hospital Association, shrinking state budgets and the below market reimbursements of Medicaid make it increasingly difficult for hospitals to meet their obligations, passing along the difference to all other patients. Uninsured individuals with chronic illness exacerbate the situation. The North Mississippi Medical Center in Tupelo collected only 5 percent of the $16 million it billed in each of the past three years to uninsured patients, and after a lawsuit claiming it discriminated against the uninsured, it now must provide free or discounted care to patients with incomes up to four times the federal poverty level ("Hospital Gives Uninsured a Break," *USA Today*, August 8, 2004). Considering that nothing is really "free," programs like

**Table 8.3   Main Risk Factors for Chronic Disease in Mississippi;
Mississippi State Department of Health**

■ **Smoking:** Smoking is the single most important modifiable risk factor for
CVD/CHD. In 2002, more than one quarter (27%) of adult Mississippians
were smokers. In 2003, about one quarter (23%) of Mississippi high school
students smoked cigarettes.

■ **High Blood Pressure** (Hypertension): Approximately 644,000 Mississippi
adults are now estimated to have hypertension. In 2001, the prevalence for
hypertension increased to 31% from 28% in 1990.

■ **High Blood Cholesterol:** In 2001, the percentage of adult Mississippians
reporting a high blood cholesterol level stood at about 31%.

■ **Lack of Regular Physical Activity**
  • In 2001, four of five (81%) adult Mississippians were not physically active on
    a regular basis (at least 5 days per week, at least 30 minutes per session).
  • More than half of Mississippi adults are sedentary: they report no leisure
    time physical activity or only irregular physical activity. In 2001, 33% of
    Mississippi adults reported no leisure time physical activity.
  • In 2003, more than 15% of Mississippi high school students did not
    participate in any vigorous or moderate physical activities during the past
    seven days.
  • In 2003, more than 54% of Mississippi high school students watched 3 or
    more hours of TV per day on an average school day.

■ **Being Overweight / Obese**
  • Mississippi ranks number one—the highest in the nation—in obesity. In
    2002, 36% of adult Mississippians were overweight (BMI between 25 and 30;
    27% were obese (BMI 30 or more).
  • In 2003, almost one-third (31%) of Mississippi high school students reported
    that they were overweight, or at risk of being overweight.

this are funded by higher health care costs for everyone else. According to the American Medical Association (AMA), Mississippi is also
one of 12 "crisis states" for rising malpractice insurance due to an active plaintiff's bar and big rewards paid by sympathetic juries.

Is the difference in longevity between Utah and Mississippi due
to the difference in health care dollars spent? What causes high expenditures but poor health? Look closely at Utah and Mississippi and
you observe that structural variables play a major role in reducing
health care costs. Attacking health care costs without analyzing what
factors lead to "good health" is comparable to a physician identifying
and treating symptoms rather than diagnosing and treating the un-
derlying disease.

Health: Within Our Control

How much do our daily habits—like diet and exercise—affect our risk for developing cancer? According to the American Cancer Society, one third of the 550,000 cancer deaths occurring in the United States each year could be prevented by eating a healthy diet, being physically active and not smoking—all behaviors that consumers control.

"Eat your veggies," your mother may have told you—and she was right! Not only are fruit and vegetables filling and naturally low in fat, the vitamins, minerals, fiber, and antioxidants they contain reduce the risk of heart disease, stroke, cancer, diabetes, and even age-related cataracts. Substituting vegetable oils (like canola and olive) and choosing lean meats and low-fat dairy products is likewise beneficial. To take full advantage of these benefits, nutritionists recommend eating antioxidant-rich foods over supplements, particularly fruit and vegetables with the most color.

As a parent, would you be alarmed to discover the school your child attends is located on a toxic dump exposing them to serious health risks? Ironically, few parents seem to be aware, let alone concerned, that foods crammed with fat and sugar are being ingested from lunch kits and school cafeterias daily. Frequently schools are paid by food manufacturers to offer chips, soda pop, and other products that are generally unhealthy. There are exceptions where parents, school officials, and food manufacturers have taken leadership to insure students receive healthy alternatives, but many schools resist change on the basis that students prefer junk foods. Many children are in fact habituated to unhealthy foods, and most often, children have learned their poor food choices from parents. If society is concerned about childhood health, then children must be taught to make healthy choices and parents must be part of that process. If parents are concerned about the physical health and well-being of their children—shouldn't that also include the food they eat?

The U.S. Department of Agriculture estimates that a healthier diet could prevent at least $71 billion per year in medical costs, lost productivity, and lost lives. The cost of treating diabetes, depression, cancer, heart disease, joint disease, trauma, birth defects, and a host of other illnesses could be reduced dramatically if consumers made better choices.

A Company of Steel

Every company faces the challenge of soaring health care costs, but Ohio-based Worthington Industries, one of the nation's leading steel companies, is doing something about the problem. Like most companies, Worthington requires employees to pay an increasing portion of health insurance premiums, but unlike most firms, those who participate in its "Healthy Choices" program pay less.

Employees who enroll in this voluntary program are screened for excessive weight, blood pressure, cholesterol, blood sugar, and other symptoms. Those found to be at moderate or high risk of lifestyle-induced illness must agree to health counseling to receive a discount on their insurance costs. To keep their discount, they must show progress in dealing with their health issues. Worthington's CEO, John P. McConnell, has said, "If you don't want to do it, it's fine with us, but you're going to have to pay more premium dollars because you're costing us more."

Since the 1970s, Worthington has invested in employee gyms, fitness classes, smoking-cessation clinics, and health fairs, but few employees participated. McConnell observed, "We were helping people who already had a mindset to go exercise or work out, but we weren't reaching the people we needed to." The company then hired Gordian Health Solutions of Nashville, Tennessee to design and administer a wellness program and announced it would charge employees $25 a month for insurance coverage ($50 a month for family coverage) unless they signed up. Companies that make health programs mandatory typically get 70 to 80 percent participation in contrast to voluntary programs that get 15 to 20 percent participation. At Worthington Industries, 2,500 of its 3,600 eligible employees (69%) enrolled.

Successful programs are not based simply on cost-shifting, but improving health behaviors and changing lifestyles of workers. Gordian estimates that companies save, on average, $1.69 for every dollar they spend on its fees in the first year. Gordian designs programs that now cover 500,000 employees for a variety of employers including Corning, Dow Chemical and the state of Virginia. In the long run, these programs are expected to reduce significantly the costs of health care for employees, employers and the nation. The most important benefit, of course, is that consumers live longer, healthier lives.

Curative Medicine vs. Public Health vs. Personal Health

Curative medicine often produces life-extending remedies for specific ailments that have already occurred, but most increases in longevity are associated with health-promoting, public health factors such as ample food supply, sanitation, public safety, education, vaccinations and other structural factors that prevent widespread illness. Lifestyle choices including a balanced diet, exercise, and abstinence from tobacco and other health-threatening substances play a major role in preventing (and fighting) disease.

Search for the decline in traffic-related traumatic injuries and costs of treating them and you'll find answers in seat belts (and laws enforcing their use), air bags, cycle helmets, better-designed highways, guard rails and safety markers, driver education and stricter sentences for driving under the influence of drugs and alcohol. Both clean drinking water and proper sanitation reduce the spread of infectious diseases. Abstinence from risky behaviors dramatically lowers the costs of treating HIV, performing abortions and overcoming substance abuse. Design changes in toys, sports equipment, clothing, stairs (and code regulations concerning their placement), security devices and many other products directly affect the costs of health care, especially for younger consumers. Future good health and longevity depends partly on parents teaching the fundamentals of good personal health. Children must be taught to look both ways before entering a street, to wash their hands after blowing their nose, to stretch before exercising, to eat nutritious food in appropriate quantities at appropriate times, to get adequate sleep and a host of other personal health practices that become a way of life.

Analyzing and promoting health-facilitating choices and creating a "health culture" for the nation is essential to the "miracle cure" for lowering health care costs, a process described in Chapter 9 that offers huge potential for lower costs and improving health. Money can't buy you love, according to a popular song. Money doesn't buy good health either. That requires changes in lifestyles, mostly personal practices that cost very little money.

CHAPTER 9

Obesity and the "Miracle Cure"

"It is not the mountain we conquer, but ourselves."
—Sir Edmund Hillary, first to
summit Mt. Everest (1953)

The Centers for Disease Control and Prevention (CDC) has declared obesity an epidemic, the nation's second leading actual cause of death and a primary factor in many others. Today, about 127 million American adults and 9 million children and teens are considered overweight or obese and 58 million live with serious obesity-related health conditions. Obesity is not only a direct cause of illnesses such as cancer, high blood pressure, heart disease, diabetes, stroke, and osteoporosis, it seriously exacerbates all other medical conditions. Fifteen co-morbid conditions are scientifically established to be the result of obesity with direct health care costs exceeding $100 billion per year, according to the American Obesity Association.

In addition to the direct costs of treating obesity-related diseases, hospitals increasingly must purchase extra-large gowns and blood pressure cuffs as well as expensive, reinforced wheelchairs, beds, stretchers, toilet seats, and other equipment to accommodate patients weighing up to 800 pounds. The U.S. health care system currently has no means of recouping such extra costs, meaning all health care consumers must pay. Spending on obesity-related medical costs reached an estimated $75 billion in 2003, of which half was paid by taxpayers through Medicare and Medicaid. Private employers incur an additional $13 billion through increased absenteeism, lost productivity, and the cost of replacing disabled workers. "Patient lifting" accidents are the number one source of job-related injury for nurses and other health care workers, resulting in millions of dollars in workers' compensation claims. These are all reasons why a successful war on health care costs begins with the battle against obesity, which begins with the public health initiative to have all people acquire good diet and exercise habits.

A Lethal Lesson from a Fatal Flight

January 8, 2003 was no different than any other morning for U.S. Airways Express Captain Katie Leslie and First Officer Jonathan Gibbs. They knew the flight would be full, but the clear sky and crisp winter air meant smooth flying for the 30–minute flight 5481 from Charlotte, North Carolina to Greenville-Spartanburg, South Carolina.

Just prior to departure, Leslie completed the standard dispatch form indicating the plane's total weight was 17,118, or two pounds short of the limit. Per airline policy, she used prevailing estimates for passenger and bag weights and adjusted the fuel weight for her taxi to the runway. As Leslie positioned for takeoff, she joked with Gibbs about a friend who brought Krispy Kreme doughnuts to a wedding. Then, with clearance from the tower, Leslie pushed the throttle forward and proceeded down the runway.

Thirty-seven seconds later, the unthinkable occurred. After lifting off the runway, the aircraft continued into a steep nose-high attitude. To bring the aircraft level and avoid a stall, Leslie pushed her entire weight on the yoke, yelling to Gibbs, "Help me!" Gibbs, also pushing the yoke, shouted an expletive over the glaring warning siren. Leslie screamed through her microphone to the control tower, "Oh, my God, we have an emergency!" In a desperate move, she pulled the throttle back and a child cried, "Daddy" as the plane fell into a nearby hanger, killing Leslie, Gibbs, and their 19 passengers in the explosion that followed.

The plane used that day was a Beech 1900, a twin-engine turboprop. With a maximum takeoff weight of 17,120 pounds, the distribution of a few hundred extra pounds could make a big difference in the aircraft's center of gravity. Post-crash studies of passenger and bag weights indicate that the prevailing weight and balance estimates used by Leslie were too low and that the aircraft was actually overweight by 100 to 300 pounds. Moreover, an examination of passenger seat assignments revealed that those sitting in the back of the plane weighed 500 pounds more than those up front, shifting the center of gravity to the rear of the aircraft. This incident provided a painful lesson that Americans are bigger than they used to be, leading the FAA to raise the "average" weight of a passenger (with carry-on) by 10 pounds to 190 pounds in the summer and 195 pounds in the winter and requiring the 15 largest airlines periodically to weigh passengers to determine if standards are still correct.

The airline industry has grappled with the problem of obesity for a number of years. In 2000, airlines paid an additional $275 million to purchase 350 million extra gallons of fuel to carry more obese passengers, resulting in an additional 3.9 million tons of carbon dioxide released into the air, according to the *American Journal of Preventive Medicine*. To survive, some airlines have eliminated bulky magazines and serving trays or replaced metal seats with lightweight plastic. One industry leader, Southwest Airlines, recoups its costs by charging obese passengers for a second seat. While some would say this practice is unfair, consider not only the added fuel costs and environmental consequences of flying heavier airplanes filled with larger passengers, but also the effect on safety. What can the health care system do to recoup its costs?

What Is Obesity?

Fighting obesity starts with identifying the problem. Obesity is defined by excess body fat, not weight alone. Commonly measured by a ratio of weight to height called the Body Mass Index (BMI), detailed in Exhibit 9.1, a BMI of 25 to 29 is considered overweight and a BMI of 30 or more indicates obesity. Typically a woman 5'5" weighing 180 pounds or a man 6'0" weighing 221 pounds would be considered obese. The relationship between excess body fat and BMI is influenced by sex and age, with women and senior citizens more likely to have a higher percentage of body fat than men and youth.

Exhibit 9.1   How to Calculate BMI (Centers for Disease Control and Prevention, 2004)

$$BMI = \frac{(\text{Weight in pounds}) \times 703}{(\text{Height in inches}) \times (\text{Height in inches})}$$

For example, a person who weighs 220 pounds and is 6 feet 3 inches tall has a BMI of 27.5.

$$\frac{220 \text{ lbs.} \times 703}{(75 \text{ in.}) \times (75 \text{ in.})} = 27.5$$

Because 27.5 is between 25 and 29, this individual would be considered overweight.

The History of Obesity

For centuries, the greatest problem facing most people has been the opposite of obesity; it's been finding enough food to survive. Look at the paintings of the great masters and it is apparent that throughout history, the only people who escaped the scarcity of daily sustenance are the privileged few. The rotund monarchs of medieval paintings might not be considered glamorous by today's standards, but at a time when ordinary people struggled to find enough calories to survive, fat was "in." In fact, obesity was once such a symbol of power and affluence that French King Louis XIV padded his body to look more imposing. Later during the French Revolution, obesity inspired the rallying cry, "The People Against the Fat." Today obesity crosses all economic and social levels but is more common among lower socioeconomic groups. And whereas the fat man was once seen as hypersexual, like Falstaff, now he is seen as asexual, like Fat Albert.

Why Obesity Grew in the United States

For much of its early history, the United States was an agrarian society. The requirements of farm life kept people lean, burning thousands of calories a day in tough, manual labor. Calories burned were often greater than calories available to eat and as a consequence, being underweight and experiencing hunger were the problems, not obesity. When the United States evolved into a manufacturing economy in the twentieth century, the use of machines and automation required fewer calories than the rigors of farm life, yet due to a more reliable food supply and greater personal income, people also tended to eat more.

With the emergence of the twenty-first century knowledge economy and "desk jobs," the need for calories has dropped even lower but calorie consumption continues to increase. Facing long, stressful days in the office, people prefer to ride to work rather than walk and they spend their leisure time watching spectator sports. Farm and factory work didn't allow much time for snacks, but in many office buildings today you'll find doughnuts, soda pop machines, and lobby coffee carts serving hyper-caffeinated, sugar-charged beverages. More people have more money, and what better way to reward themselves than with food? As a result, the United States has become a nation of mostly overweight and obese people.

Although Americans don't need to consume more calories, government subsidies of grain encourage them to do just that. Between 1970 and 2000, the amount of corn produced per capita in the United States increased 75 percent from 20 to 35 bushels and thanks to technology, farmers who once grew 30 bushels per acre now yield 130 (*New York Times,* October 12, 2003). It's not difficult to figure out where all those extra calories have gone. Some are exported but most find their way into food—cereal, breaded nuggets, corn syrup, chips, and the like. As a result, since 1977, the average daily intake of calories has jumped by more than 10 percent and an extra 200 calories per day results in a weight gain of more than 20 pounds per year unless exercise is increased to compensate. Bigger farm yields are beneficial to the economy so long as the additional corn becomes fuel for gas tanks rather than padding around people's waists.

Once fat is deposited it takes significant food (calorie) deprivation to mobilize and burn the stored fat. To remove one pound of fat containing 3,500 calories, the body's food intake must be below need by 3,500 calories. If daily food intake is too severely restricted in an effort to lose the fat quickly, however, the body responds by entering "starvation" mode burning the fat at a slower rate.

Trying to mobilize and burn deposited fat is accompanied by many of the same problems as trying to quit smoking. The process of burning fat causes changes in body chemistry, causing many individuals to feel sick. Just as inhaled tobacco smoke halts the discomfort of nicotine withdrawal, eating food ends the discomfort of burning fat. Emptied fat cells also remain for a long time and are ready to absorb the next excessive food intake as fat. Once fat is deposited in large quantities, losing it becomes complex and often requires medical supervision. The difficulties of large weight loss are generally poorly understood or appreciated by the general public.

Does Size Matter?

If your life matters, then your size also matters. A 40-year-old nonsmoking woman's life will be cut short by an average of 3.3 years by being overweight and 7.1 years by obesity, according to the American Heart Association. Obesity has been compared to wearing a "down parka" except that the excess fat changes the entire physiological makeup of the person. Obesity changes how the body handles the storage and utilization of nutrients (sugar, oxygen, hormones, fat-soluble vitamins, etc.), the ways the heart functions, insulin is produced, blood is distributed to tissue, oxygen is absorbed, and metabolic byproducts are removed. In many ways, obesity creates a toxic internal environment in which some tissue is "starved" of vital nutrients. Over time, these physiological changes lead to grave consequences.

Metabolic syndrome, defined as three or more of the following five factors: high triglycerides; low "good" cholesterol; high blood sugar; high blood pressure; and a big waistline, precedes more deadly repercussions. Overweight and obesity account for 20 percent of all cancer deaths in women and 14 percent in men, meaning 90,000 cancer deaths could be prevented each year if Americans maintained a normal, healthy body weight (*New England Journal of Medicine*, Vol. 348, No. 17: 1625–1638). Obesity increases the risk of several cancers, including cancers of the breast, colon, endometrium, esophagus, and kidney. Cancer growth can also be stimulated by mechanical processes in which abdominal obesity leads to acid reflux into the esophagus, and hormonal processes, in which obesity increases circulating levels of estrogen and insulin. The effects on breast cancer are compounded because obesity not only increases the risk of developing the disease in the first place, but the presence of fat makes cancer cells more difficult to find and treat, thus increasing the risk of death.

Despite overwhelming evidence that obesity may lead to cancer, a 2002 American Cancer Society survey concluded that just one percent of Americans identified "maintaining a healthy weight" as a way to reduce cancer risk. In a society in which weight has been associated more with appearance and self-esteem, there's work to be done in increasing awareness of being overweight and obese as a life-or-death problem.

> *Solution to America's "Two Trillion Dollar Crisis": Health and governmental organizations should increase communication relating obesity to poor health and high health care costs.*

Morbid vs. Simple Obesity

Clearly in discussing the topic of obesity, consideration must be given to the factors that cause an individual to be overweight, whether they are psychological, physiological, genetic, or cultural. Someone who realizes they could stand to lose the 10 or 15 pounds they've gained in the past few years due to a more sedentary lifestyle and neglect of their diet is in a much different situation than someone who has been considerably overweight much of their lives and has attempted diets, exercise, and other weight-loss programs with great frustration and limited success.

While medical dictionaries define the former as "simple obesity," or caloric intake that exceeds energy expenditure, the latter is considered "morbid obesity," or "obesity sufficient to prevent normal activity and physiological function, or to cause the onset of a pathological condition." Generally, the "morbidly obese" weigh 100 pounds over their ideal weight. The number of people in this category has quadrupled from one in 200 adults in 1986 to one in 50 today.

Simple obesity is best tackled through diet and exercise, but treating morbid obesity involves a critical balance of the causes and effects of obesity. For instance, obesity has been linked to depression as both a cause and effect. While it is possible that a patient's depression might subside if they lost weight, unless their depression is treated first, they may be unmotivated to make the necessary changes in their lives. Medical treatment of morbid obesity must therefore consider "the whole person." On the surface it may seem that the solution to the obesity epidemic is to get people to eat less and exercise more, but this change is very difficult to accomplish and research is critical to address the issue successfully. That's why the National Institutes of Health funding for obesity research has increased from $378.6 million in 2003 to $440.3 million in 2005 (*LabMedicine,* October, 2004).

Could You Be Infected with an Obesity Virus?

Although obesity occurs when the body burns fewer calories than it consumes, the attitude that obesity is the consequence of slothful overindulgence has fallen to an understanding that obesity is a disease and that it's possible some people are predisposed to fat.

In the last few years, scientists have uncovered evidence that many chronic health conditions are caused by infections. Three different microbes have been linked to clogged arteries, and peptic ulcers, once believed to be the product of high stress and a poor diet, are now known to be caused by the bacterium *helicobacter pylori*. Researchers at the University of Wisconsin believe that a virus related to the common cold may likewise be a factor in obesity (*International Journal of Obesity,* August, 2000).

Studies uncovered infection with the adenovirus-36 virus in 20 to 30 percent of the obese population compared to five percent of the lean population, and tests of laboratory animals showed that those infected with the virus not only weighed an average of seven percent more than uninfected animals, their bodies also contained twice as much fat. When the amount of food consumed was controlled for both groups, eliminating appetite as a factor, researchers concluded that the virus either decreased energy expenditure or increased the number of fat cells, allowing their bodies to store more fat. This doesn't mean that all obesity is caused by a virus, but the results do suggest that infection plays an important role. That's why researchers are working on a vaccine that in the future might reduce the probability of obesity or counteract the effects of the virus. Until then, counting calories counts.

Surgical Remedies for Obesity

The most aggressive method of treating morbid obesity is bariatric surgery, including gastric-bypass which creates a much smaller stomach and rearranges the small intestine, greatly reducing how much food can be absorbed. The number of procedures has increased nearly sevenfold from 20,500 in 1996 to 140,640 in 2004, according to the American Society of Bariatric Surgery. Surgical procedures cost around $26,000 and are typically reserved for patients who have tried other remedies without success. Studies show that patients who have the surgery not only live longer on average than those in similar health who do not (*Journal of the American College of Surgeons*, October, 2004), they also lost 67 percent of their excess weight (*Annals of Surgery*, September, 2004).

Experts believe that bariatric surgery improves long-term survival in many patients, but the procedure is not without risk. There have been some deaths reported as an immediate result of the surgery as well as complications including leakage, bowel obstruction, stricture, bleeding, ulcers, gallstones, and infection. If patients do not change their diet and lifestyles, they may end up with protein or vitamin and mineral deficiencies. In fact, if they keep eating, they might not lose any weight at all. Of course, it could also be possible that patients who elect the surgery are in better general health than those who do not, and because surgery is performed in conjunction with diet, exercise, and other lifestyle changes, the actual benefits may be fewer than they appear.

Communicating Effectively to Obesity Segments

In a society filled with seemingly endless choices—from the cable television channels consumers watch to the websites they browse—marketing is rarely effective to "mass markets." Instead, effective marketers identify and appeal to specific groups of people, described as "segments" or "niches" with similar behavior, often measured on the basis of demographics (age, income, ethnicity and geography), psychographics (activities, interests and opinions) and "lifestyle" variables. Communication aimed at changing diet and exercise habits must be directed to segments that might be described as:

1. Consumers who are normal weight
2. Consumers who are overweight
3. Consumers who are obese

If communication is to be effective in changing behavior, it must recognize the existence of *selective perception,* which refers to the way people are exposed to, comprehend, and retain information on the basis of their attitudes, opinions and previous behavior. The practical implication is that normal weight consumers will listen to and believe information about the problems of obesity, but overweight and obese consumers will tend to avoid and dismiss such information, sometimes even taking offense to it.

Overcoming Selective Exposure: The Arkansas Model

Selective exposure explains that consumers are unlikely to have contact with communication that conflicts with their beliefs and behavior. Overcoming selective exposure is therefore the first component of an effective strategy to combat obesity.

Where is antiobesity information found? It's mostly in wellness journals, at the gym and in *Cooking Light* magazine—information sources not likely to reach many obese people. Unless marketing programs are carefully designed to include the television programs, magazines and activities that impact overweight consumers, we shouldn't expect these segments to be exposed to information that might cause them to consider changing their thoughts and actions. Moreover, unless such communications are approached with compassion and sensitivity, obese people will likely avoid them altogether. Obese consumers have suffered negative comments and insensitivity to the difficulty of changing their conditions, feelings of inadequacy and diminished self-worth for falling short of media-defined "ideals," and in some cases, blatant job and social discrimination. If obesity were easy to prevent or cure, most would have changed years ago.

Forced exposure is one way to break though the communication barrier created by selective exposure. Some employers, such as Worthington Industries (described in the previous chapter) accomplish this with mandatory health screenings that include weight and BMI measurements. To qualify for employer contributions to employee health insurance, obese employees are required to complete an educational program that provides factual information on the relationship between obesity and health, similar to what occurs when employees have alcohol or other substance abuse problems.

A broad program to force exposure to obesity information has been initiated by the state of Arkansas under the leadership of Governor Mike Huckabee. At 5'11" and nearly 280 pounds, Huckabee was told by his doctor that he had Type 2 diabetes and would likely not live another 10 years. A highly disciplined individual, Huckabee resolved to lose the weight and through a rigorous diet and exercise, lost 105 pounds in 10 months—completely curing his diabetes. Now he's focused on helping everyone else in Arkansas do the same.

More than 61 percent of adults in Arkansas are overweight or obese, a rate that increased by 80 percent between 1991 and 2002. In addition, 14 percent of Arkansas' youth are overweight, 34 percent do not get enough exercise, and 19 percent are current smokers. Although Arkansas is a state of only 2.7 million residents, its Medicaid program pays over $3 billion a year for 660,000 participants. Seventy-seven percent of Medicaid funds are spend on chronic illness, the bulk of which is caused by poor choices in diet, physical activity, and tobacco use.

Recognizing the unhealthy state of Arkansas citizens, while acknowledging initiatives currently in place, Governor Huckabee determined that more needed to be done. He asked that policy makers, health professionals, and business leaders partner to change the culture of health throughout the state. In 2003 the Arkansas Legislature passed Act 1220 requiring yearly BMI measurements on all public school children. Reports are sent to the parents of each child, along with information about the health risks of obesity. This program is a two-front attack on the problem of selective exposure in that it provides information to the people most able to control the problem of childhood obesity—the parents—while also forcing information upon an adult population likely to be obese.

Huckabee also created "Healthy Arkansas," a comprehensive effort to clearly define specific areas where behavioral changes can lead to healthier citizens. "Healthy People" goals attack obesity, physical inactivity, and tobacco use. Efforts include enlisting the media in disseminating information and presenting awards to encourage the participants.

Solution to America's "Two Trillion Dollar Crisis": State governors and legislators should lead the war attacking obesity and poor health, learning from the experiences of Arkansas and other programs that focus on preventing childhood obesity.

Overcoming Selective Comprehension: "Got Milk?"

Selective comprehension occurs when consumers are exposed to information but selectively interpret it consistent with their existing beliefs and behavior. Masses of consumers read or hear information that vitamin-rich, high-fiber foods are beneficial to their health, but they selectively interpret the information to conclude they don't taste as good, are too expensive, or require too much effort to adopt.

Researchers at the University of Missouri-Columbia have created vegetable-based meat substitutes that are remarkably similar to the texture, appearance and feel of actual meat, duplicating the taste of beef or chicken so effectively that 80 percent of consumers in blind taste tests choose them over the real thing. However, millions of Americans never try such products because they perceive they are not as tasty as high-fat, high-cholesterol alternatives, and they selectively interpret taste on their belief that "if it's healthy, it must taste bad." Overcoming selective comprehension requires behaviorally-based and precisely-executed communications programs, often involving creative visual materials, memorable slogans, celebrity endorsements and the paired associations of new products with existing products that are already preferred by consumers.

The sales of healthy foods were so unhealthy for so many years that many of America's marketers considered them a lost cause. An example of effective attitude change is the "Got Milk" campaign. After decades of decline, the milk industry increased per capita consumption by associating milk with athletes, rock stars (such as Aerosmith) and other celebrities, set in the context of compelling graphics coordinated along with the simple, but memorable slogan, "Got Milk."

It's not likely that creative programs such as these will be developed by the government, but when public health breaks the barrier of selective exposure by forcing awareness of the consequences of obesity and poor health, it opens the door for private industry to develop creative programs that overcome selective comprehension by consumers.

Although antiobesity advocates would like to blame the consumer packaged goods and fast food industries for contributing to the obesity epidemic, these same industries may also be a vital part of the solution. Once private industry understands the impact of poor health on America's ability to compete in a global market and consumers demand products that will help them improve their own health, firms such as Kraft, Nestlé and Kellogg's with years of marketing experience will be best positioned to promote healthy lifestyles. In response to market trends, Wendy's transformed fast food with its selection of pre-packaged salads, going from minimal market share to 12 percent of sales. McDonald's responded with its own healthier initiatives, giving away five million pedometers to weight-conscientious adults and adding fruit and milk options to its children's meals. These and other "change agents" can be an ally in the war on obesity and health care costs as they create more products and marketing programs that break through the selective perception of America's attitudes and behavior about health, eating healthy, and being healthy.

Overcoming Selective Retention: Enlist Change Agents

Selective retention is the process of reverting to behavior consistent with existing attitudes and behavior. This means that even if consumers are made aware of the need to be healthy and they comprehend how to achieve such behavior, they will tend to revert to their unhealthy habits. As discouraging as this seems in fighting the war on health care costs, it underscores the need for comprehensive programs that reinforce good behavior built upon long-term goals and strategies rather than quick-fix solutions and fad diets. Because their relationship with consumers is most complete and most enduring, the most likely "change agents" in accomplishing these strategies are probably employers. As America moves toward consumer driven health care, employees and employers both have a huge stake in reducing health care costs.

> *Solution to America's "Two Trillion Dollar Crisis": Creating consumer awareness of health care costs will attract private industry to develop products and marketing programs that reduce obesity and enlarge market segments willing to eat better to be healthier.*

Obesity and Diet

Atkins™, South Beach™, Beverly Hills, Low Carbs, Low Fat, Slim-Fast™, and Suzanne Somers—the list of popular diets goes on and on. While it's not our intention to evaluate the latest diet fad and there is evidence that each can be effective in losing weight initially, the real issue is how to keep the weight off over time. The National Weight Control Registry, which tracks the "secrets" of individuals who have lost at least 30 pounds and kept it off for at least a year, has determined that regardless of how people lose weight initially, those who keep it off do so by limiting fat rather than carbohydrates. Possible reasons low-carb diets fail is that people replace carbohydrates with fat rather than protein and that people lack the discipline to adhere to strict dietary guidelines for extended periods of time. According to the American Institute for Cancer Research, a common sense approach is best—"eat a balanced diet weighted toward vegetables and fruit, reduce portion sizes, and increase physical activity."

The Miracle Pill

An article in *Harvard Magazine* (March-April 2004 Volume 106, No. 4) describes so well a "miracle pill" to prevent many of America's health problems and costs, that we've chosen to reproduce its encapsulation as a solution to America's "Two Trillion Dollar Crisis."

> *"In the bottle before you is a pill, a marvel of modern medicine that will regulate gene transcription throughout your body, helping prevent heart disease, stroke, diabetes, obesity, and 12 kinds of cancer—plus gallstones and diverticulitis. Expect the pill to improve your strength and balance as well as your blood lipid profile. Your bones will become stronger. You'll grow new capillaries in your heart, your skeletal muscles, and your brain, improving blood flow and the delivery of oxygen and nutrients. Your attention span will increase. If you have arthritis, your symptoms will improve. The pill will help you regulate your appetite and you'll probably find you prefer healthier foods. You'll feel better, younger even, and you will test younger according to a variety of physiologic measures. Your blood volume will increase, and you'll burn fats better. Even your immune system will be stimulated. There is just one catch. There is no such pill. The prescription is exercise."*

It's a prescription that many fail to fill, perhaps citing the reason, "I don't enjoy exercise." And until recently, the economic impact of avoiding exercise was minimal because "someone else" paid for the physical consequences. Exercise avoiders might also defend their behavior on the basis that they are not overweight or "it doesn't matter" if they are. Yet, the benefits of exercise extend beyond the benefits of reducing weight.

Vigorous exercise has been shown to stimulate the body's immune system and other defenses, lowering the risks of many types of cancer up to 40 percent. Women who engage in 1¼ to 2½ hours of brisk walking per week have an 18 percent lower incidence of breast cancer compared to inactive women. Likewise, more than 90 percent of Type 2 (adult-onset) diabetes can be prevented or delayed by exercise. Studies indicate that walking 30–45 minutes a day lowers the risk of Type 2 diabetes by 30 to 40 percent while lowering a diabetic's risk of dying from heart disease by 40 to 50 percent. By raising levels of HDL or "good" cholesterol, exercise substantially reduces the risk of heart attacks and strokes. In addition to warding off infection by stimulating the body's immune system, research now indicates that muscle-building exercise can strengthen the skeletal system to the point that broken arms and broken legs are less like to occur as people cross the age 50 threshold.

If you're planning a romantic weekend with your partner, don't forget to pack your running shoes. In an environment saturated with ads for Viagra, Cialis and Livitrol, it's easy to conclude that the solution to health problems such as erectile dysfunction (ED) is to pop a pill, but studies indicate a regular program of exercise is far more effective. According to researchers at Harvard University, exercise enhances the relaxation response necessary for an erection and improves vascular reactivity to stimulation. Vigorous exercise leads to vigorous sex, for both men and women.

Whether its heart failure, strokes, cancer, ED, diabetes or osteoporosis, many health problems can be prevented and sometimes reversed by exercise. If the thought of going to a gym or buying an exercise bike turn you off, other activities count such as washing the car, vacuuming the house and raking leaves. Or, how about walking? It's free, requires no special equipment or training, it can be enjoyed at any age, and it's easy to integrate into your existing lifestyle. Rather than taking the elevator or an escalator, what about taking the stairs? Instead of emailing a colleague, what about visiting his or her office? Or, when shopping, what about parking farther away and returning your grocery cart to the front of the store?

At one time, recommendations called for a program of moderate exercise at least three times per week. More recent studies, however, emphasize daily activity at levels high enough to cause a sweat. If you're looking for a way to get started, consider the acronym FITT, described in the following table.

Table 9.1   The Exercise Prescription: FITT
Source: American Diabetes Association

Frequency:	3–5 times per week (increasing to most days)
Intensity:	Moderate Intensity: 55 to 70% of age-predicted maximal heart rate; or perceived exertion of 3–5 on a scale of 0 (easiest) to 10 (hardest) effort; 3 miles/hour
Time:	30–45 minutes (shorter, more frequent bouts in those who haven't inactive; increase to 60 minutes per day)
Type:	Low-impact activities such as walking, cycling, or water exercise.

We don't all have to be groupies of Jack LaLanne, the physical fitness guru who celebrated his 90th birthday with television appearances, a day of push-ups (he still holds the world's record for the greatest number of push-ups) and an evening of exuberant dancing. But if you prefer a romantic evening in bed with your partner instead of a hospital bed, your best bet is to follow his example of eating plenty of fresh fruits and vegetables and getting plenty of exercise.

Solution to America's "Two Trillion Dollar Crisis": A national program with representatives from health, education, commerce and other leaders should be convened to document and communicate the advantages of exercise to health care costs and recommend a coordinated program for America's employers, schools and other organizations.

Treating the "Whole Person"

"Father of preventive medicine" Kenneth H. Cooper, M.D., who added an "s" to turn the adjective "aerobic" into the noun "aerobics" and launched a worldwide fitness revolution, is as passionate about his faith as he is his fitness. "Unless you're spiritually fit and physically fit, you don't know the real joy of living," he told the *Dallas Morning News* (November 14, 2004).

Although other physicians initially balked at Dr. Cooper's idea of providing stress tests to patients and adapting a fitness regime designed for astronauts to "ordinary people," he felt it his personal mission to promote a simple-to-understand concept of wellness that combined exercise, proper nutrition, and supplements including vitamins and antioxidants. (Some of Cooper's observations are summarized in Table 9.2).

Table 9.2   **"Father of Aerobics" Kenneth H. Cooper's observations on how to achieve and maintain good health. (Source: *Dallas Morning News*)**

Exercise—in conjunction with weight control, proper nutrition, and adequate supplementation—is the foundation of a good wellness program.

A person who is physically fit is less likely to be depressed and will have a better self-image, a more positive attitude towards life, and fewer bodily complaints.

The best aerobic exercises are cross-country skiing, swimming, jogging, cycling, and walking. Among those, just about anyone, regardless of age or gender, can exercise safely and effectively.

The first step of any exercise program is to avoid inactivity. Collectively, 30 minutes of activity most days of the week have been show to have health and longevity benefits.

Weightlifting and muscle-building exercises must be done in conjunction with, not in place of, a primary aerobic program.

Today the Cooper Aerobics Center in Dallas, Texas attracts "princes and presidents, preachers and pro athletes" who receive individual and group wellness training. In addition to advising large corporations such as Frito-Lay on the development of "healthy" products, the wellness center provides one-on-one treatment ranging from physician-supervised physicals to residential weight-loss programs and pampering spa treatments. According to one patient, the campus is quite impressive but the program is tough and thorough. "By the time you show up for your annual physical at 7:00 in the morning, have what seems like a gallon of blood drained out of you, all manner of poking/feeling on and in your body, are stripped naked and dunked in a tank, moved to the brink of heart attack on a treadmill, you are left with a blinding headache from exhaustion, lack of food and no morning coffee meaning you get to spend the rest of the day lying in bed trying to recover."

Despite the rigors of the program, this patient and many others look forward to tracking their progress over the years. All successful marketers know the key to long-term success is building enduring relationships with consumers. Cooper accomplishes this by providing patients with a lifelong program that helps them increase longevity and realize "harmony in life," based on Cooper's philosophy of "keeping God at the top, family second, and work third."

There is growing evidence that spirituality can provide a sense of purpose and belonging that gives individuals the strength to overcome adverse circumstances and the hope to envision a better tomorrow. That's why many "self-help" programs, based on the successful model of Alcoholics Anonymous, encourage participants to believe in, and seek the support of a "higher power." People who pray often feel that they have more control over their circumstances, causing them to adopt more positive changes in their lives. Research also shows that individuals involved in faith communities have stronger immune systems and recover from illness faster, have less incidence of depression, heart disease and hypertension, and have greater self-esteem and more fulfilling interpersonal relationships—all causing them to live longer on average than people who profess no faith.

Science has yet to provide a complete explanation of faith's positive benefits, but evidence the benefits exist is overwhelming. According to Duke University psychiatrist Dr. Harold Koenig, "the degree of hope and emotional strength afforded by religion to some older adults may far exceed that obtainable from other sources."

Summary for Health Cost Reduction through Better Health

What's the "miracle cure" to health care costs? It's personal responsibility, accompanied by personal accountability. Starting with the 10 percent of children age two to five and ending with the 55 percent of the Medicare population currently overweight or obese, America faces a health crisis that left untreated will lead to astronomical rates of stroke, heart disease and diabetes in the future. The result will be even more national resources absorbed by health care, lower productivity, lower longevity, and a lesser quality of life for all Americans. Consumer driven health care is successful when consumers do their part to achieve and maintain good health and a Health Savings Account makes it profitable when they do.

CHAPTER 10

Who Will Solve the Problem?

"With the right information and the right incentives, capitalism creates very good solutions."
—Dr. Francis J. Crosson, Executive Director,
Kaiser Permanente Physicians Group

"What is the manager's job? It is to direct the resources and efforts of the business toward the opportunities for economically significant results. (And not at the most nagging problems!) What is the major problem? It is fundamentally the confusion between effectiveness and efficiency that stands between doing the right thing and doing things right."
—Peter Drucker, *Harvard Business Review*

Consumer driven health care is gaining momentum faster than a runaway train—regardless of whether consumers board voluntarily or have no choice but to simply hang on. This book is not an analysis of what *should* happen to the U.S. health care system. Rather, it's a description of what *is* happening as consumers pay a greater proportion of their health insurance premiums and face rising co-pays and other out-of-pocket expenses. Survival in a global economy forces all Americans to become conscripts in the war on health care costs, with the choice being to fight or lose their jobs.

The changes proposed in this book will not come easily or on their own. When consumers assume control of their expected, normal health care expenditures, they will force health care institutions to provide the products and services they want, at prices they are willing to pay, creating an open consumer marketplace for health care and a new paradigm for understanding America's health care system. The result will be greater efficiency, higher quality, increased satisfaction, and better personal health.

Critics may protest the transition to consumer driven health care, claiming many consumers are unable to make informed decisions about health care. A change from the current system of "someone else" paying health care bills can be compared to a child leaving a home where parents paid the bills and made most of the buying decisions to becoming independent adults paying their own bills and deciding themselves how to budget expenses to fit their resources. Once consumers begin to see how better health care choices affect their wallets or HSAs, they will seek information to maximize the value of their health care dollars. Some consumers will adjust to the change and some probably will not, but even consumers who are least able to understand and adapt to the new environment will still benefit from the improved delivery models brought about by those who do.

"Marketing Is Everything And Everything Is Marketing"

Fundamentally, the transition to consumer driven health care is a *marketing* solution to America's "Two Trillion Dollar Crisis." In his best-selling books, Silicon Valley thought leader Regis McKenna observes that through marketing, technology and society shape and reshape each other ceaselessly, like tireless meshing gears in a perpetual motion machine. Organizations that survive and thrive realize the truth of McKenna's conclusions that "marketing is everything and everything is marketing." To understand what that means requires a careful definition of a frequently misunderstood word—marketing.

Marketing is often confused with selling. Although *selling* involves getting customers to buy a firm's products or services (using techniques such as advertising, promotions, and networking), *marketing* is best understood as *changing the organization* to produce what consumers will buy, at a price they are willing to pay (and hopefully still generate a profit).

Marketers are sometimes accused of manipulating people or at least of influencing them. That's an accurate understanding of marketing, providing it's understood *which* people are manipulated or influenced by marketing. The role of effective marketing is *not* to manipulate consumers. The role of marketing is to manipulate or influence the producers of goods and services. In order to survive, producers must understand the behaviors, needs, wants, and desires of consumers while also communicating effectively to consumers, "we sell what you are willing to buy." Consumers, in turn, reward the firms that provide the greatest satisfaction with a share of their hearts, minds, and wallets.

Market-based capitalism contrasts sharply with centrally planned economies in which "someone else"—usually the government—decides what's best for people and coordinates production and distribution of products and services based on social policy, without regard as to whether consumers are truly satisfied. In third-party controlled health care systems, "someone else"—government, employers and their insurance companies—decides what's good for consumers. The problem is that when third-party payers negotiate directly with health care providers, the needs of actual users of the health care system (consumers) become secondary.

When consumers begin to pay for much of their own routine health care, they will demand a voice in what services they receive; how much they will cost; and when, where, and how they receive them. With the enormous incentive provided by HSAs, consumers will be rewarded when they make good choices. In consumer driven health care, consumers will also reward health care providers (hospitals, physicians, and others) that manage their operations efficiently and effectively communicate why their products are better than those offered by other providers.

The "driver of change" in consumer driven health care therefore is consumers with money to spend, and marketing is the tool for bringing about a health care system that truly meets consumer needs (at a price they can afford). As described in previous chapters and summarized in Exhibit 10.1, the changes may include new delivery models, new payment systems, new funding sources (especially the HSA), greater information access, and better lifestyle choices.

A Three-Component Solution to America's "Two Trillion Dollar Crisis"

The solution to America's "Two Trillion Dollar Crisis" encompasses the three primary components of the health care system including curative medicine, usually provided by health care institutions, preventive

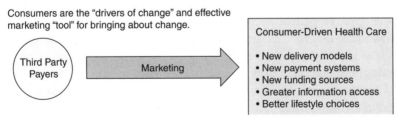

Exhibit 10.1   The Enabling Process for Consumer Driven Health Care is Marketing

medicine, including public health initiatives to influence personal health behaviors, and the individual choices consumers make regarding their own personal health.

While the third-party payer system has shifted a disproportionate number of health care resources to curative medicine (health care providers in the business of "sickness care"), consumer driven health care will restore balance to each component as follows.

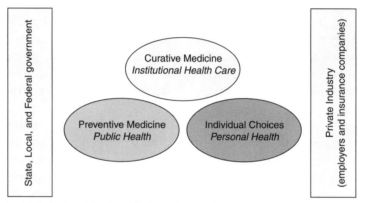

Exhibit 10.2   The Health Care System in the United States consists of three components that interact with each other, directed in the past by third-party payers

Curative Medicine

The "entry point" to the health care system for many individuals is not prevention or wellness, but rather to seek treatment or relief for a disease or illness that has already occurred. Curative medicine consists of the institutional providers of health care products and services that rescue and resuscitate the multitudes drowning in the "river of poor health" (described in Chapter 8). Whether illness is caused by genetic predisposition, environmental factors, or personal choices, institutional health care has responded with innovative, often effective and usually expensive methods to cure the maladies of an increasingly obese (and now increasingly aging) population.

Curative medicine has been highly profitable for biotech research firms, pharmaceutical and medical device manufacturers, insurance companies, hospital management companies, and others in the "business" of health care. Generally speaking, physicians and other health care providers are still among the highest paid professionals in America. There's big money to be made in curing people who are sick, even among institutions that are officially classified as not-for-profit.

Historically, the customers of these health care providers have not been the actual patients (consumers), but rather, the employers, insurance companies, and government agencies that paid the bills. Like any business that strives to please its customers, health care providers have accommodated third-party payers, allowing them to dictate what treatments will be administered, to which patients, at which times, and in which locations. Health care providers have also had to adapt their accounting and record keeping systems to meet the demands of these "customers." Meanwhile, the actual users of the health care system (consumers) complain about being unable to schedule an appointment, having to drive across town and sit in a waiting room, completing multiple forms and spending hours on the telephone tracking down claims information, physicians who don't take time to listen, and unsatisfactory clinical outcomes. Moreover, any savings from health care providers becoming more efficient accrue to the third-party payers providing an incentive to further restrict consumer choice and reduce quality to the minimal level of care that prevents a lawsuit. Health care providers struggle with below-market reimbursement, complex billing procedures, and the inability to exercise medical judgment without first consulting the payer's rules. Health care providers who have built their organizations on meeting the needs of third-party payers now face a dilemma as a substantial portion of health care—normal, routine medical expenditures—is shifted to individuals, turning consumers into customers.

Because of the role of third-party payers, consumers in the past have not been well-informed or skilled in making decisions about which providers to choose, the prices they charge, which treatments are the most effective and least costly, and how to prevent illness. Now that consumers are taking control of a greater percentage of their health care expenditures (and are rewarded in their HSAs for spending those dollars most efficiently), they have an enormous incentive to become informed, skilled purchasers of health care forcing revolutionary changes in health care providers of the types described in Chapter 6.

Institutions that survive will need to change both the efficiency with which they operate and the marketing programs required effectively to attract and to retain "satisfied customers." There can be no doubt that health care providers of all types will want to be effective in communicating the advantages of their solutions. It is therefore safe to conclude that the "marketing" of health care products and services (not to be confused with "selling") will be changed dramatically.

The Tough Transition for Traditional Health Care Providers

Who will be the winning health care providers in the future? Business history teaches that the more successful an organization has been in the past, the more likely it is to fail in the future. The reason is that success is so rewarding that successful firms are unlikely to change the activities that made them successful until a crisis disrupts their way of doing business. Then, it is often too late because the competition that forced the crisis is already years ahead. Health care providers face a brave new future in consumer driven health care. The best health care providers will learn from, and benchmark against, the best marketing practices from nearly every other industry. They will probably look to the lessons learned from banks and brokerages, airlines such as Southwest and JetBlue, and retailing success stories ranging from Wal-Mart and Target to Chico's and Limited Brands.

The health care institutions least likely to be affected by consumer driven health care are those that provide health services beyond the scope of routine or everyday health care. Examples include the Mayo Clinic, Cleveland Clinic and other regional or even international facilities offering highly specialized care. They may even benefit if enough consumers switch to high deductible policies providing greater coverage for catastrophic illness—especially if insurance premiums decrease sufficiently to reduce the number of uninsured consumers.

The most difficult transition, however, will be for providers of routine or everyday health care, especially if they are locked into an infrastructure with high fixed costs. Examples include many health maintenance organizations (HMOs), general-purpose hospitals and primary care physician practices. The promise of HMOs was that by managing the total health care needs of an individual or family, practicing preventive medicine in a highly efficient format, the total costs of health care would be reduced. Except for smoking cessation and substance abuse programs, the promise has been mostly unfulfilled as most HMOs changed little about health care except creating large administrative bureaucracies with highly paid executives who must turn a profit. The philosophy of "we will make all health care decisions for consumers" is fundamentally opposed to consumer driven health care, in which consumers make health care decisions themselves. The incentives also differ, with HMOs being more profitable by providing less care or placing greater restrictions on care.

Among HMOs, one of the oldest and most respected is Oakland, California-based Kaiser Permanente. With origins dating back to the 1930s, when industrialist Henry J. Kaiser created a foundation to provide health care for his construction and shipyard workers, Kaiser is now the nation's largest private-sector provider of health care, employing more than 11,000 physicians and 135,000 other workers in 30 hospitals and hundreds of clinics. Viewed as "dependable, low cost coverage for working-class people," Kaiser serves more than eight million members in nine states and the District of Columbia, with 70 percent of its members in California.

Kaiser is both an insurer and provider with employers typically paying fixed yearly fees for each member, regardless of how much care is provided. Although a not-for-profit organization, Kaiser's annual revenue exceeds $25 billion with operating margins of five percent. Its facilities tend to be large with a reputation for practicing an impersonal, regimented style of medicine that limits patient choice. Kaiser's commitment to information technology, efficient business processes and cost-effective management of chronic diseases, however, achieves relatively low total costs for its core customer base—large employers. A survey of health care costs in 15 metropolitan areas conducted by Hewitt Associates, a human resources consulting firm, found that average health care costs per employee were lowest in the San Francisco area, where about 35 percent of insured persons are Kaiser members.

Marketing in consumer driven health care means that Kaiser and other HMOs must now offer products and services that meet the health care needs of different population segments, pricing them according to usage, cost of service, actuarial risk, and other factors. Dr. Francis J. Crosson, executive director of the affiliated Permanente Medical Groups has said, "Our future has to be to compete on quality, offering people demonstrably better care and better value" (*New York Times,* October 21, 2004).

As a result, Kaiser's conducts marketing campaigns that target the needs and interests of different user segments. One such group is "Health Seekers" who take accountability for their health, lead a healthy lifestyle, and want a relationship with providers that encompasses health education, wellness, prevention and even access to alternative, complementary therapies. Another is "Cost Driven Consumers," price-sensitive young males who do not have a relationship with a single physician, who desire access and convenience, and who are not adverse to the HMO delivery model if it provides sufficient "value" to justify the premiums.

Individual physicians and group practices face a similarly tough transition, especially if they depended on insurance companies to pay in the past for patient care. They must make the transition from high-overhead offices with staffs accustomed to completing insurance forms to simple administrative procedures based on cash, debit cards or checks. The problem arises because of the gradual transition; a large number of "private pay" patients paying from their HSAs should not be expected immediately. The dilemma facing physicians is how to price in the interim. Should they continue charging the high prices required to handle insurance claims or should they charge the lower prices required to attract cash customers? Or should they have two different prices for each category of customer? (Medicare, Medicaid, and other third-party payers often prohibit physicians from offering discounts or charging lower prices than what these programs pay). If physicians don't have a lower price for HSA customers, they run the risk of losing their best paying (usually younger and more affluent) patients to alternative providers organized around the cash-pay model.

Currently a challenge exists because of the "overlay" of HSAs and traditional, first dollar coverage. Many physicians will not see new patients unless they have health insurance. The high deductible policy required for an HSA is health insurance (a PPO, HMO, or other policy); however, routine doctor's visits not covered by the deductible will still be paid out of pocket. In order for the visit to count towards the deductible, and perhaps towards incentives the physician receives for seeing "in-network patients," the physician's staff still submits a claim to the insurance company for the visit. Of course, the claim is denied due to the deductible, and the physician then bills the consumer. Until separate processes are developed, there is no additional time saved for consumers paying by HSA, although computers and automated systems may speed some of the paperwork. Just as some businesses have shunned credit card companies that charge higher processing fees, it's likely some physicians will start to express a preference for providers with streamlined processing, or to patients paying cash.

How to make the transition from third-party reimbursement is fundamentally a marketing issue and marketing is not a topic taught in most medical schools. From a societal perspective, the best solution is a two-price system, because its existence stimulates more rapid diffusion of HSAs. From the physician's perspective, a two-price solution is probably also the best solution if the goal is retain their present patients and reduce the risk of their migrating to alternative providers. In fact, some physicians have successfully implemented "cash only" practices, causing consumers to file their own insurance paperwork if they require reimbursement. For many physicians, the ideal of a practice free of insurance forms and managing a large office staff probably is a scenario worth pursuing.

The Future of Health Insurance Providers

Insurance companies face a particular dilemma in consumer driven health care. When consumers switch from expensive traditional first dollar health insurance to the types of low cost, high deductible health plans required to contribute to an HSA, insurance company revenues drop dramatically. That's great for consumers and employers, but imagine the problem facing an insurance company CEO or CFO who must now tell financial analysts to expect declining revenues and profits for the foreseeable future! The more expensive health care is in America, the more profitable are health insurance companies who make money from the actuarial profits derived from underwriting health risks, fees charged to employers and the government to process claims and other paperwork, as well as returns on the assets accumulated as reserves. The double-digit increases in revenues that insurance companies and their investors have come to expect in the past are open to question in the future.

Two solutions are possible for health insurance companies. One solution is to be aggressive in writing new types of policies, such as high deductible coverage, with more customer appeal in an HSA environment. There are advantages to insurance companies in offering high deductible policies. Not only is the risk of catastrophic illness actuarially predictable, but high deductible policies don't require the costly bureaucracy to approve and reimburse claims under first dollar coverage. In addition, high deductible policies with HSAs make health insurance affordable for a greater number of Americans, opening new markets and creating new revenue streams. Last, many people who are healthy and willing to go uninsured due to the high cost of first dollar coverage will be more open to buying high deductible coverage, particularly with the tax savings of an HSA. These consumers are less likely to file claims than individuals who require first dollar coverage, resulting in lower underwriting expense.

The companies that develop and implement effective marketing strategies may capture enough market share from competitors to retain or increase profitability. Less efficient or less effective firms will be driven from the market. That's exactly the desired effect of consumer driven health care: replace inefficient firms with more productive firms, helping everyone—employees, employers and the economy. Everyone that is, except investors and employees in inefficient firms.

A second marketing solution is for health care insurance companies to change their primary source of profits from underwriting and claims processing to asset management. That's likely to happen as financial institutions compete with each other to be the depository for HSA accounts. Some banks and brokerage firms already are aggressively marketing HSAs and the numbers can be expected to grow rapidly. For insurance firms with a substantial health insurance portfolio, expect considerable activity in the creation or acquisition of banking subsidiaries to serve as depositories for HSA assets. As competition intensifies, firms should also start allowing "sweep" accounts that invest HSA balances in higher-yielding mutual funds, which of course are managed for a fee by the financial institution. For consumers, this means they may need to deal with different financial institutions than the familiar ones of the past, a process most people don't find comforting. The firms with the most effective marketing are, of course, the ones likely to win the battle for customers' minds and wallets.

Preventive Medicine and Public Policy

The toughest solution to America's "Two Trillion Dollar Crisis" may be prevention. Although the benefits to preventive medicine including greater longevity and improved quality of life are within reach—

unlike money spent on curative medicine—the results are not seen for many years. Moreover, to the bulk of health care institutions focused on treating illness, there is no immediate profit in prevention, and funds spent on public health must compete with other politically-expedient programs including education, transportation, and public safety. As illustrated in Chapter 8, good health and lower health care costs can be achieved through comprehensive efforts to have people acquire good lifestyle habits, but the solutions require complex and competent marketing programs to succeed.

First, there must be research that determines and documents the programs most likely to be effective. Second, change leaders must understand the significance of such research well enough to fund implementation of the research findings. Third, change leaders must have both the long-term perspective and communication skills needed to persuade voters and their congressional representatives that the long-term returns from preventive health care justifies spending over other needs. Ultimately, the most effective prevention strategy is found in the choices individual consumers make about their own personal health.

Individual Choices and Personal Health

In the past century, individuals had little financial incentive to be responsible for their own health choices because "someone else" paid the bills when consumers became ill. As a result, personal health is declining for vast numbers of Americans. Lifestyle-induced illness, especially obesity, and other unhealthy decisions lead to lost productivity, shortened longevity and reduced quality of life. In consumer driven health care, however, consumers who take personal responsibility for the health decisions are winners who can take their savings to the bank, preparing for the future with an HSA.

Marketing performs an important function when it improves quality of life and prevents premature deaths, but the only people who can do something about the costs of unhealthy lifestyles are the American populace. In essence, it's your civic duty—you'll be your own worst enemy if you don't! "Sign me up. Where do I start?" may be the response of some readers. Your local YMCA or fitness center is probably the best place to start, as you may have concluded after reading about the "miracle cure" in Chapter 9. There are more health care dollars to be saved using this approach than all of the "miracle cures" that modern medicine can create.

Solutions to America's "Two Trillion Dollar Crisis"

Throughout each chapter of this book, you've read italicized conclusions as "solutions" to America's "Two Trillion Dollar Crisis." When each is implemented, it provides insight on how to save American jobs—potentially your own—and solve many of the health care problems that burden this country. Hopefully, you have given each of the solutions considerable thought. Some solutions require action by you as a consumer, some require political leadership which consumers can encourage and reward, and some require fundamental changes in the business models of health care providers. Some solutions contribute relatively small amounts to solving the "Two Trillion Dollar Crisis," while others bring about hundreds of billions of dollars of savings. There are many more solutions that are possible, of course, and hopefully you will come up with some of your own. We encourage you to share these ideas with your friends, family, and co-workers, and use them to start a public dialogue on how to transform America's third-party funded "sickness care" system into consumer driven health care.

In the best-selling business book of the last century, *Built to Last*, authors Jim Collins and Jerry Porrous report that the most successful business organizations develop, communicate and implement visionary values. It is values—shared views of goals and behavior—that allow some corporations to rise above others, recognized and rewarded by consumers. Will American political, professional, business and union leaders arise with similar abilities to articulate and lead America to a health care system with visionary values based on prevention of disease rather than curative medicine? At the very least, consumer driven health care is more likely to create an environment in which the electorate understands the importance of creating such a system and rewarding leaders who emerge to lead the battle in America's war on health care costs.

The Future Is Here

Many people desire one big answer to problems, but usually the bigger the problem, the greater number of answers required to solve the problem. That's why we've examined indirect costs, direct costs, new delivery models, prevention and personal accountability. Consumer driven health care, by changing how health care is paid for, changes the entire power structure of the health care delivery system placing you in charge!

This book is not intended as merely an interesting read, but rather, a call to action. The solutions proposed in this book could reduce total health care costs as a percentage of GDP dramatically, protecting your job and restoring the nation's competitive position. Nothing is more likely to bring about change than asking consumers to pay a portion of their own health care costs and rewarding them in an HSA when they do.

The alternative to consumer driven health care is nightmarish. Not only could you end up with no job and no health insurance, but you could also face an early death with nobody to take care of you. Whether you are a consumer, businessperson, government official, health care provider, student, or anyone else interested in ways to reduce health care costs, consumer driven health care is upon us. Are you ready for it?

Modern Achievements in Medicine and Public Health

Advances in medical science and public health have extended the lifespan of the average human being from 24 years during the Roman Empire to 46 years in the early 1900s to nearly 78 years today, with an increasing percentage of people living into their 90s. Thanks go to the hard work, education, skills and intuition of those on the frontline of patient care as well as those less visible in libraries, laboratories and classrooms.

Collective scientific research pushes our knowledge and understanding of the human body to new frontiers. What follows is a summary of the many advances that have increased not only the length of our lives, but the overall quality and enjoyment as well.

On the top of our list must be **public health and prevention** including:

- Vaccinations
- Motor vehicle safety
- Occupational safety and health
- Control of infectious disease
- Understanding of diet and nutrition
- Family planning and pre-natal care
- Treatment of drinking water and processing of sewage
- Recognition of the harms of tobacco use

Within this category, special emphasis must be placed on **mass immunization,** which has eradicated the serious disease of smallpox and controlled epidemics of others such as diphtheria and polio in developed countries.

Evidence-based medicine requires that physicians evaluate patients based on the facts at hand, developing a plan of treatment that integrates the physician's clinical expertise with the latest clinical research findings. Rather than try old folk remedies and hope they work without complication, physicians practice on the basis of **efficacy**—defined as the "power or capacity to produce a desired effect"—with all efforts focused on bringing about the best outcome given the patient's unique profile.

An application of these concepts is **rational drug design** in which researchers study various compounds to determine which ones produce the desired results. Before pharmaceuticals are made available for prescription, they are thoroughly tested for safety and effectiveness—protecting us from anecdotal remedies that might be harmful. An extension of chemically-based pharmaceuticals is **molecular genetics,** which enables us to "unravel" DNA—the genetic blueprint of life—and learn how to treat or prevent many stubborn diseases.

Understanding how **vitamins and minerals** work is another important advancement, as it has helped us realize the function and health benefits of different types of foods. Likewise, understanding **cardiovascular risk factors** has taught us the relationship between fats, cholesterol, and exercise in preventing heart disease, stroke, diabetes, and kidney disease as well as promoting wellness. And when heart disease does occur, we've mastered a range of treatments ranging from minimally invasive angioplasty to open heart bypass surgery.

Surgery, made humane by **anesthesia,** has also enabled those blinded by cataracts to see again and has given new life to old arthritic joints through high-tech prostheses. In just a few short years, **organ transplants** have become routine. Some day it's possible that we'll clone tissue or perhaps entire organs that can be stored and used as needed. Anti-rejection techniques are increasing the likelihood of success and making transplants a common part of our health care system.

Early identification and treatment of cancer prolongs the lives of those affected by this dreaded killer. We can already pinpoint and treat some cancers successfully and we're learning more all the time. New drugs and drug delivery systems are in the pipeline that will help to turn the tide in the fight against this killer disease.

Last, **diagnostic technology** has allowed us to identify signs of disease and intervene, often stopping disease in its path. We couldn't measure someone's blood pressure at the turn of the last century.

Today, we have machines that can explore the entire inner-body without a single intrusion.

Of course, there are many additional medical achievements that could be mentioned, and the possibilities for future achievement are almost limitless.

The burning question addressed by this book is ***how do we pay for that future?***

About the Authors

Roger D. Blackwell, Ph.D. has taught over 65,000 students during 39 years at The Ohio State University. In addition to writing 28 books including *Consumer Behavior* (used throughout the world in multiple languages), he has served as a director of numerous public and private companies. Currently a professor of marketing and logistics at the Fisher College of Business of Ohio State, he received B.S. and M.S. degrees from the University of Missouri and a Ph.D. from Northwestern University.

Thomas E. Williams, Jr., M.D., Ph.D. is a distinguished open heart surgeon who has served in multiple hospital leadership positions and on medical missions to developing nations such as Viet Nam, Rwanda, and Malawi. As a faculty member at The Ohio State University, he has contributed significantly to the medical literature. Dr. Williams earned a B.S. from Princeton University, M.S. and M.D. degrees from The Ohio State University, and a Ph.D. from Northwestern University.

Alan A. Ayers, MBA, MAcc, is Director of Consulting Services for Roger Blackwell Associates, a marketing strategy and advisory firm located in Columbus, Ohio. He has served as a project manager and consultant for global clients and has been involved with multiple technology start-up companies. Mr. Ayers earned a B.A. with Distinction from the University of North Carolina at Chapel Hill, an MBA from the University of Mississippi, and a Masters in Accounting from the Fisher College of Business of The Ohio State University.

Index

A

accelerated education programs, 93–94
adenovirus-36 virus, 158
administrative costs, 58–60
aerobics, 166
airline industry
    crisis in, 103–106
    obesity issues and, 152–153
Albrecht, Karl, 107, 111
Albrecht, Theo, 107, 111
Aldi (Albrecht Discount), 106–108
allocation of resources, 8–10
    by centralized planning, 9
    by lottery, 9
allopathy. *See also* curative medicine;
        institutional health care
    alternatives to, 47–48
alternative medicines, 48
    ayurveda, 48
    homeopathy, 47–48
alternatively skilled health care
        providers, 96–97
American Association for Graduate
        Medical Education, 90
anesthesia, 184
Apollo Hospital, 50
arbitration for malpractice claims,
        74–75
Arkansas, obesity program, 160–161
arnica, 46
ayurveda, 48

B

baby boomer effect, 27–28
bariatric surgery, 158–159
benefits, health care, 4
best practices, global, 35–36, 51, 55
billing data, universal format for, 63
Blackwell, Roger D., 8, 67
Blue Cross Association, 124–125

Blue Shield, 124–125
Body Mass Index (BMI), 153
branding, 17. *See also* marketing
budget planning, 8
Buffet, Warren, 4
Built to Last (Collins and Porrous),
        52, 180
business
    health care costs, coping with, 20
    health care costs, impact on, 4–5
    productivity, increasing, 20–21
    profit generation, 17–18
"Buy American" campaigns, 19

C

California, pay or play law, 126
Canada Health Act (CHA), 39–40
Canadian health care system, 39–42
cancer
    identification and treatment of, 184
    Mississippi death rates, 145–146
    obesity and, 156
    risk factors, 148
cardiovascular disease (CVD)
    death rates by county, 143
    Mississippi death rates, 145
    risk factors for, 184
care provided by family members,
        10, 124
cash-pay model, transition to, 176. *See
        also* consumer driven health care
Catholic Hospital West (San
        Francisco), 61
centralized planning, 9–10
centrally planned economies versus
        market-based capitalism, 170–171
children
    personal health fundamentals,
        teaching, 148, 150
    preventing obesity in, 161

China
  labor cost advantages, 46
  productivity of health care
    system, 38
  urbanization of, 35
Christenson, Clayton, 102
chronic disease risk factors, 147
Church of Jesus Christ of Latter-day
    Saints (LDS), 142–144
cigarette smoking
  decline in, 11
  as disease risk factor, 145–147
clinical data, universal format for, 63
clinical mistakes, reducing with
    technology, 61
Clinton, Bill, 99–100
Clinton, Hillary, 99–100
co-payments
  for government-insured patients in
    Germany, 45
  increasing, 126
  requirements for, 24
  in Singapore, 53
Collins, James C., 52, 180
communication. *See also* marketing
  exercise-related, 166
  obesity-related, 156, 161, 163
  to patients, 74
consumer beliefs, 2–4, 8
consumer driven health care
  consequences of, 122
  definition of, 2
  disruptive and dislocative strategies
    of, 14
  efficiencies of, 15, 100
  health care availability, 32
  health care provider transition to,
    174–177
  job protection from, 32
  as marketing solution, 170–171,
    175–176
  momentum of, 169
  producers, roles and responsibilities
    of, 67
  transition to, 14–15, 135, 169–170
consumer lifestyles. *See also* lifestyle
    choices

  cultural influences on, 11
  as determinant of health care
    costs, 11
consumers
  control of personal health, 5
  as drivers of health care, 171
  health care costs, pain of, 68–69
  health care costs, shifting to, 24
  health care dollars, maximizing, 170
  health care prices, awareness of, 132
  as informed purchasers of care, 173
  online access to medical data, 61–62
  voice of, 171
contingency fee limits on malpractice
    claims, 74
continual process improvement, 98–99
contracts, affect on costs and cost
    control, 12
contractual releases for health care
    services, 74
Cooper, Kenneth H., 166
Cooper Aerobics Center, 167
corporate fraud, 79–80
Crosson, Francis J., 175
culture, influence on health and health
    care standards, 10–11
curative medicine, 6, 139–140. *See also*
    institutional health care
  longevity and, 140
  versus personal health, 149–150
  resources focused on, 171–172
customer-centricity, 67
The Customer Comes Second
    (Rosenbaum), 119
customer satisfaction, by low-cost
    suppliers, 104–106
customer service, focus on, 23

D
da Vinci, Leonardo, 6–7
data mining, 78
deductibles, requirements for, 24. *See
    also* high-deductible insurance
    policies
defensive medicine, 12. *See also*
    malpractice insurance
  costs of, 72

demand chains, 67
  leader capabilities, 67
demand in health care, 8
  increases in, 17, 83
  for nurses, 86
Deming, Edward, 36, 98
department stores, inefficiency of,
  102–103
depression, obesity and, 157
diabetes in Mississippi, 146
Diagnostic Related Groups (DRGs), 9
diagnostic technology, 184–185
diet
  healthy choices in, 148
  obesity and, 163
diet fads, 163
direct costs of care, 83
  hospital care and clinical services,
  83–84
discharge orders, efficient use of, 65
disease prevention through exercise,
  164–165
disposable personal income (DPI),
  gains in, 21
Drucker, Peter, 4
drug design, 184
Duke University Health System, 110

E
economic systems
  purpose of, 7
  supply and demand relationship, 8.
    See also demand in health care;
    supply of health care personnel
economics, market-driven versus state-
  controlled, 56
efficacy, as basis for care, 184
efficiency
  improving, 65–66
  information sharing and, 98–99
  of low-cost suppliers, 104–106
  in resource use, 64–65
  retail model for, 106–111
  of Singapore's health system,
  54–55
  of specialty hospitals, 114
elderly health care in Singapore, 54

emergency rooms
  paperwork burden of, 58–59
  in specialty hospitals, 115
employees
  benefits, costs of, 4–5
  cross-training, 23
  health care costs, sharing with
    employers, 24, 125–126
employer-sponsored health plans, 3–4
  employee contributions, 125–126
  for healthy lifestyle promotion, 54
  as input cost, 18
  wellness programs, 148–149
employers
  as buyers of health care, 5
  health care costs, sharing with
    employees, 24, 125–126
  retirement policies, changing,
  30–31
European Union, health care systems of
  (European Model), 44–46
evidence-based medicine, 184
exercise
  benefits of, 164
  FITT (frequency, intensity, time,
    type) of, 165
  as miracle pill, 163–166
expense control, 107

F
faith, health benefits of, 167
family members, care provided by,
  10, 124
fast food industry, as promoter of
  healthy lifestyles, 162
fat
  BMI and, 153
  burning, 155
  limiting intake of, 163
federal government, as buyer of health
  care, 5
fee-for-service system, 41
  reimbursements of, 45
females, in physician profession, 86
first-dollar coverage, 9
  disadvantages of, 121–124
  high-deductible policies and, 126

and HSAs, overlay of, 176–177
   reducing evils of, 125–127
FITT (frequency, intensity, time, type)
   exercise program, 165
flexible spending accounts (FSAs), 128
   features of, 134
foreign professionals, attracting and
   retaining, 87, 91–92
fraud, 75–81
   compliance strategies, 77–78
   corporate, 79–80
   costs of, 75, 77
   definition of, 76
   deterrence of, 78
   eliminating, 77–79
   scams, 80–81
   in third-party payer systems,
   76–77
Freedom Just Around the Corner
   (McDougall), 56
frivolous lawsuits, 12
From Mind to Market (Blackwell), 67
From the Edge of the World (OSU Press),
   35, 52

G
gatekeepers, cost-inefficiency of,
   48–49
general hospitals, plight of, 111–113
general wards, 43–44
Generation X, 27
Generation Y, 27
Germany
   health care system, 44–45
   health care system productivity, 38
Gibbs, Jonathan, 152
global best practices, 35–36, 51, 55
global markets, selling in, 35
global sourcing, 35
global thinking, 15, 34–36
   attributes of, 35
globalization, 18–19
   job migration in, 17–18
Gordian Health Solutions, 149
"Got Milk?" campaign, 162
government malpractice insurance, 74
Greenspan, Alan, 4, 28

gross domestic product (GDP)
   gains in, 21
   percentage spent on health care in
   Canada, 41
   percentage spent on health care in
   Germany, 45
   percentage spent on health care in
   Hong Kong, 42
   percentage spent on health care in
   India, 47
   percentage spent on health care in
   Singapore, 52
   percentage spent on health care in
   United States, 2–3, 37–39, 58
group practices, transition to
   consumer driven health care,
   176–177

H
Hahnemann, Christian Friedrich
   Samuel, 47
health and well-being
   cultural influences on, 10–11
   goal of better health, v
   personal responsibility for, 38. *See*
   also personal health
health care
   affordability of, 54
   indirect costs of, 57, 70, 72–73, 81
   personal responsibility for, 46. *See*
   also personal health
   as right versus benefit, 4
   savings for, 30. *See also* Health
   Savings Accounts (HSAs)
   spending on, 2–4
health care benefits, 4
health care costs
   comparison with other indicators, 22
   economic growth, effect on, 2–4
   expenditures per worker, 20
   lowering, 5
   obesity-related, 151
   rises in, 1–2, 19–20
   sharing between employers and
   employees, 24
   by source of funds, 1960–2000,
   58–59

health care crisis
   components of, 171–172
   solutions to. *See* solutions to health
      care crisis
health care expenditures
   in 2004 in United States, 1
   percentage distribution, 112
   as percentage of U.S. GDP, 2–3,
      37–39, 58
health care professionals
   alternatively skilled, 96–97
   productivity of, 84
   shortages of, 25–26, 83–90
   at specialty hospitals, 119
   transition to consumer driven health
      care, 174–177
   unionization of, 85
health care resources
   allocation of, 8–10
   polarity in distribution of, 15
   supply of health care personnel, 8,
      25–26, 83–90
health care standards, cultural
      influences on, 10–11
health care system
   access to care measures, 52
   components of, 6–12
   inefficiency of, 5
   productivity of, 37–39
   quality and efficiency of, 2, 5, 52
   quality measures, 52
health insurance. *See also* insurance
   high-deductible policies, 24–25,
      126–127, 177–178. *See also*
      Health Savings Accounts (HSAs)
   premiums, rises in, 125
   providers, future of, 177–178
Health Insurance Portability and
      Privacy Act (HIPAA), 63–64
health maintenance organizations
      (HMOs)
   goals of, 174–175
   Kaiser Permanente, 175–176
health messages
   forced exposure to, 160
   selective comprehension of, 161–162
   selective exposure to, 159–161

selective perception and, 159
selective retention of, 162–163
health outcomes, structural variables
      and, 142–147
health-promoting activities
   lack of, 6
   teaching of, 48
health reimbursement arrangements
      (HRAs) , features of, 134
Health Savings Accounts (HSAs), 15,
      127–130
   administrative costs of, 59–60
   advantages of, 128
   asset management for, 178
   contributions to, 128–129
   demand for, 132
   distributions, 128
   eligible medical expenses, 137–138
   employer contributions to, 129
   features of, 134
   and first dollar coverage, overlay of,
      176–177
   funding of, 29
   as incentive to stay healthy, 129–130
   portability of, 129
   reimbursements, 128
   for retirement medical expenses, 129
   selecting, 133
   sweep accounts, 178
   tax status of, 127
   threats to, 130–131
HealthSouth Cooperation, 79–80
heart disease
   death rates by county, 143
   Mississippi death rates, 145
   risk factors for, 184
heart transplants, origination of, 36
helicobacter pylori, 157
herbal remedies, 46
high blood cholesterol, 147
high blood pressure, 147
high-deductible insurance policies, 126
   advantages for insurance providers,
      177–178
   HSAs and, 24–25, 127
home health care, paperwork burden
      of, 58–59

homeopathic medicine, 47–48
Hong Kong health care system, 42–44
hospitals
    aligning goals with staff, 113, 120
    digitizing, 61–62
    general hospitals, plight of, 111–113
    general wards, 43–44
    hospital-to-physician fee ratios, 112
    labor costs, 84
    malpractice, affect on, 73
    occupancy rates, 54
    original purpose of, 124
    paperwork burden on, 59
    physician-owned, 113
    specialties, grouping of, 65
    specialty hospitals, 113–120
    working conditions in, 87–89, 111
Howard Community College fast-track
    nursing program, 26
HSAs. *See* Health Savings Accounts
    (HSAs)
Huckabee, Mike, 160–161
Hull, Walter, 141

I
immigration, health care professional
    shortages and, 87, 91
India
    advantage in labor costs, 46
    health care system, 46–50
    health care system productivity, 38
    medical tourism to, 50–51
indirect costs of health care, 57
    non-value-added costs, 70,
      72–73, 81
individual choices
    effect on health, 146
    personal health and, 53–54, 168,
      179–180. *See also* personal health
    resources focused on, 172
information sharing, 98–99
information systems, 60–61
    Radio Frequency Identification
      systems, 62–63
    at Seoul National University
      Bundang Hospital, 61–62
    smart cards, 62–63

The Innovator's Dilemma
    (Christenson), 102
inpatient surgery
    paperwork burden of, 58–59
    rates of, 54
input costs, lowering, 17–18
institutional health care, 140. *See also*
    curative medicine
    changes required of, 173–174
    customers of, 173
    versus longevity, 140
    profitability of, 172–173
institutional life cycle, 101–102
insurance. *See also* health insurance
    cafeteria plans, 24
    early programs, 124
    first-dollar coverage, 9, 121–127,
      176–177
    for-profit plans, 124–125
    good versus bad, 123
    high-deductible policies, 24–25,
      126–127, 177–178
insurance companies
    asset management functions, 178
    as buyers of health care, 5
    malpractice, affect on, 73
    transition to consumer driven health
      care, 177–178
Intermountain Health Care (IHC),
    69–70, 110, 144
    success factors, 71
inventory velocity, 107

J
Jackson, Bo, 79
Japan
    best practices of, 35–36
    longevity statistics, 37
    quality advances and efficiency
      improvements, 98
JetBlue Airways, 104–106
job migration, 18–19
job retraining programs, 26
Johnson & Johnson, 35

K
Kaiser, Henry J., 175
Kaiser Permanente, 110, 175–176

Kelleher, Herb, 111
Koenig, Harold, 167

L
labor costs
China and India advantages in, 46
as differentiator, 17–18
Labor Department statistics,
unemployment data, 21
LaLanne, Jack, 165
LASIK surgery, 36
lawyers, effect of malpractice on, 73
legal and political factors, 11–12
Leslie, Katie, 152
life expectancy, 140. *See also* longevity
variation across states, 142
life support systems, 10
lifestyle choices, 148
cigarette smoking, 11
health effects of, 146
obesity and, 11
personal health and, 150. *See also*
personal health
wellness programs and,
148–149
work/life balance, 94–96
lifestyle-induced illnesses, 1
longevity
curative medicine's role in, 140
as measure of national health,
36–37
overweight/obesity and, 155–156
lottery system, for allocation of
resources, 9
Louis XIV, 154
low-cost suppliers
consumer satisfaction by,
104–106
efficiency of, 104–106
lung cancer, 146

M
Malarkey, William, 11
Malawi, preventive medicine in, 141
males in nursing profession, 86
malpractice
affect on health care, 73
definition of, 72

malpractice insurance
cost of, 12, 90
as non-value-added cost, 70, 72–73
reducing need for, 49
malpractice suits
based on malpractice versus
malintent, 49
frivolous, 74
limits on awards, 74–75
physician practices resulting
from, 72
reducing costs of, 74–75
market-based capitalism versus
centrally planned economies,
170–171
market-driven economics versus state-
controlled systems, 56
market system, 9–10
marketing
in consumer driven health care,
175–176
definition of, 170
effectiveness of, 66–68
as enabler of consumer driven health
care, 170–171
functions, shifting to efficient
channel members, 66–67
functions of, 66
profits, increasing with, 17
role of, 170
to segments and niches, 159
selective comprehension,
overcoming, 161–162
selective exposure, overcoming,
159–161
selective perception and, 159
selective retention, overcoming,
162–163
markets, low costs and weak
competition in, 109
mass immunization, 183
mass retailers, 103
McConnell, John P., 149
McDougall, Walter, 56
McNair, Malcolm, 102
Medicaid patients, refusal of, 122
medical care, expectations of, v

Medical City, Dubai, 51
Medical Consumer Price Index
    (MCPI), 22
medical miracles, expectations of, 6
medical records
    comprehensive system for, 63–64
    paper-based, 61
medical savings accounts (MSAs), 128
medical science, advancements in, 6–7,
    183–185
medical students
    accelerated programs for, 93–94
    recruiting, 86–87, 92–94
    student debt of, 92
medical tourism, 50–51
Medicare
    deficits in, 28–30
    entitlements, unpredictability of, 28
    health care costs for employees
        on, 31
    problems with status quo, 31–32
Medicare Prescription Drug,
    Modernization and Improvement
    Act, 127
Medicare tax, 27
metabolic syndrome, 156
Mexico, health care system of, 38
Middleby Corporation, 23
minerals, 184
MinuteClinic, 110–111
mission, aligning with medical staff,
    113, 120
Mississippi, health outcomes in,
    144–147
molecular genetics, 184
Murphy, Kevin, 13

N
Natio, Mercer, 20
national health care
    in Canada, 39–42
    disadvantages of, 41–42
    funding sources, 41
    principles of, 39–40
national health expenditures, 2–3
National Health Insurance program
    (NHI), 39

New Albany Surgical Hospital
    (NASH), 115–120
New England Study Group, 99
non-value-added costs
    eliminating, 81
    malpractice insurance, 70, 72–73
Northeastern Ohio Universities College
    of Medicine (NEOUCOM),
    93–94
Not Invented Here (NIH)
    Syndrome, 34
nurses
    shortage of, 10, 25–26, 85–89
    unions of, 85
nursing care
    by family members, 10, 124
    nurse-to-patient ratios, 85
    paperwork burden of, 58–59
    training programs in, 88
nutrition
    disease prevention through, 148
    poor, as risk behavior, 145

O
obesity
    airline industry effects, 152–153
    cancer and, 156
    costs of treating, 151
    definition of, 153
    depression and, 157
    diet and, 163
    effect on health care costs, 11
    epidemic of, 151
    health messages about,
        communicating, 159
    health messages about, forced
        exposure to, 160–161
    history of, 154
    increases in United States, 154–155
    morbid versus simple, 156–157
    physician shortages and, 90
    selective comprehension of health
        messages about, 161–162
    selective exposure to health
        messages about, 159–161
    selective perception of health
        messages about, 159

selective retention of health care
messages, 162–163
surgical remedies for, 158–159
virus as factor in, 157–158
Ohio State University One-Chart
program, 61
organ transplants, 184
outpatient surgeries, growth in,
112–113
outsourcing, 1–2, 18–19
overtime
versus new hires, 18, 20
productivity, increasing with, 23
overweight/obesity. *See also* obesity
longevity and, 155–156
as risk factor, 147

P
packaged goods industry, as promoter
of healthy lifestyles, 162
paperwork
burden of, 58–60
cost-inefficiency of, 49
patient care, personnel shortages
and, 85
patient choice, 53. *See also* individual
choices
patient data
confidentiality of, 63–64
patient control over, 63–64
patients, as hospital customers, 111. *See
also* consumers
payroll gains, health care costs and,
22–23
peer group certification of malpractice
claims, 74
pensions, origin of, 29–30
personal health
children, teaching fundamentals to,
148, 150
versus curative medicine, 149–150
individual choices and, 179–180. *See
also* individual choices
lifestyle choices and, 150. *See also*
lifestyle choices
as miracle cure, 168
public health, shifting from, 142

Philips, 36
physical inactivity, 145
as risk factor, 147
physician extenders, 97
physicians
accelerated education programs for,
93–94
complaints of, 94
educational debt of, 92
foreign graduates, 91
frustrations of, 90
as hospital customers, 111–112
hospital-to-physician fee ratios, 112
lifestyle issues, 94–96
malpractice, affect on, 73
median salaries of, 96
performance-based incentives
for, 113
physician-owned hospitals, 113
reimbursement of, 45
residency rules, 90
retirement age of, 90
shortage of, 89–92
transition to consumer driven health
care, 176–177
plastic surgery procedures, origination
of, 36
polarity of trade, 102–103
poor nutrition as risk behavior, 145
Porrous, Jerry I., 52, 180
prepaid health care, 39–40
preventive medicine, 6
cost savings of, long-term, 12–13
expenditures on, 140–141
medical advancements in, 183
physician shortage, effects on, 97
profitability of, 179
resources focused on, 171–172
results of, long-term, 178–179
upfront costs of, 12
price, salaries, and productivity, 107
productivity
gains in, 21
increasing, 18, 97–99
price, salaries, and, 107
of U.S. health care system, 37–39
profits in business, importance of, 4

provider fraud, 76–77
public health
    medical advancements in, 183
    personal health, shifting to, 142
    physician shortage, effects on, 97
publicly financed health care, 39–42

Q
quality assurance, 98
quality improvement, 98
    sharing techniques of, 98–99
quality of service of low-cost suppliers,
    104–106
quasi-retirement, 30–32

R
Radio Frequency Identification
    (RFID), 62–63
Ramsay, Cynthia, 52
rational drug design, 184
recipient fraud, 76–77
Reddy, Prathap C., 50
residency
    foreign graduates in, 91
    new rules for, 90
resources, efficient use of, 64–65
restructuring worker abilities, 25–26
retail industry, polarity of trade in,
    102–103
retailers, superefficient, 106–111
retirement
    age for, adjusting, 30–31
    quasi-retirement, 30–32
right to health care, 4
Ring, Jeff, 26
risk factors
    for cancer, 148
    for cardiovascular disease, 184
    for chronic disease, 147
    cigarette smoking as, 145–147
    overweight/obesity as, 147
    physical inactivity as, 147
    poor nutrition as, 145
risks of procedures, communicating to
    patient, 74
Rolling Stones, 36
Rosenbaum, Hal, 119
Rule of Three (Sheth and Sisodia), 101

S
salaries, price, and productivity, 107
Salo, Terry, 50–51
SARS, 34–35
scams in health care, 80–81
school lunches, unhealthy foods in, 148
Scrushy, Richard, 79–80
selective comprehension, overcoming,
    161–162
selective exposure, overcoming,
    159–161
selective perception, definition of, 159
selective retention, overcoming,
    162–163
self-employment, 21
self-medication, 48
    in India, 47
Seoul National University Bundang
    Hospital, 61–62
Service Employees International Union
    (SEIU), 85
Shaw, George Bernard, 29
Shell Oil, 36
Sheth, Jagdish, 101
sickness care. *See also* curative medicine
    expenditures and focus on, 139–140
Singapore
    health care system of, 51–55
    Ministry of Health website, 54
single-payer systems, 41. *See also* third-
    party payer system
    administrative costs of, 59
Sisodia, Rajendra, 101
Six Sigma, 98–99
skilled nursing care. *See also*
    nursing care
    paperwork burden of, 58–59
small businesses
    consumer driven health care in, 24
    health care costs of, 22
    jobs created by, 21
smart cards, 62–63
smoking
    decline in, 11
    as disease risk factor, 145–147
social health insurance contributions,
    44–45

Social Security
  benefits, predictability of, 28
  deficits in, 28–30
  spending on, 28
socialized medicine, 44–46
  disadvantages of, 46
  funding of, 44–45
  rationing of procedures, 141
Society of Thoracic Surgeons,
  98–99
Soderquist, Donald, 33
solutions to health care crisis, 180
  age of Medicare and Social Security
    benefits, increasing, 31
  alternative medicines, 48
  as call to action, 181
  consumer choice for low-cost
    providers, 106
  exercise-related communications, 166
  high-deductible policies, 127
  international best practices, learning
    from, 35–36, 51, 55
  low-cost providers, purchasing
    procedures from, 51
  lowering costs of health care, 49
  malpractice suits, analyzing, 49
  medical profiles, standardizing, 63
  medical student debt forgiveness, 93
  medical students, accelerating
    education of, 94
  multiple-bed wards, 44
  nurse education, funding, 26, 89
  obesity-related communications,
    156, 161, 163
  quality improvement processes,
    adopting, 99
  self-medication, 48
  shifting costs to consumers, 24
Southwest Airlines, 104–106
  obesity-related costs, 153
specialists
  HSA payments for, 96–97
  median salaries of, 96
specialties
  grouping of, 65
  physician lifestyle differences
    in, 95

specialty hospitals, 113–115
  New Albany Surgical Hospital
    (NASH), 115–120
  opposition to, 114–115, 119–120
  transition to consumer driven health
    care, 174
specialty stores, 103
spirituality, health benefits of, 167
stock market gains, 21
structural variables, effect on health
  outcomes, 142–147
student debt forgiveness, 93–94
superefficient organizations, 106–111
supply chain management, 17,
  107, 109
supply chains
  demand chains, 67
  traditional, 67
supply of health care personnel, 8
  nursing shortage, 10, 25–26, 85–89
  shortages in, 83–90
surgery, advancements in, 184
Switzerland, best practices of, 36

T
Take Control of Your Aging
  (Malarkey), 11
technology. *See also* information
  systems
  advances in health care, 6–7,
    183–185
  consumer expectations of, 7
  as driving force of health care costs,
    49–50
  expense of, 7
  potential of, 7
  in specialty hospitals, 118
third-party payer system, 5
  consumer needs, secondary nature
    of, 171
  disadvantages of, 58
  first-dollar coverage, 9, 121–127,
    176–177
  fraud in, 76–77
  hospital-to-physician fee ratios, 112
  inefficiencies of, 60–61, 121–122
  ownership of health care system, 58

producers and consumers in, 67
rules for allocation of resources, 9
shifting away from, 14–15
transition to cash-pay model,
    176–177
tobacco use
    decline in, 11
    as disease risk factor, 145–147
Topel, Robert H., 13
traditional health plans. *See also* health
    insurance
    attributes of, 135–136

U
unemployment rate, 21
Unilever, 36
uninsureds, 24–25
    high-deductible policies and HSAs
        for, 131–132
    uncollected fees from, 146
unionization of health care
    professionals, 85
United States
    longevity statistics, 37
    market-driven economy of, 56
    obesity in, 154–155. *See also* obesity
    "sickness care" system in, 6
universal health care coverage, 42–44,
    99–100
    funding of, 42
    laissez faire regulation of, 42–43
    quality of care, 43

U.S. military medical personnel, 97
Utah, health outcomes in, 142–144

V
visionary values, 180
vitamins, 184
voluntary health insurance (VHI)
    market in Germany, 44
von Bismarck, Otto, 29

W
Wal-Mart, 33, 108–111
    "Buy American" campaign, 19
Walton, Sam, 33, 111
wellness
    economic incentives for, 129–130.
        See also Health Savings Accounts
        (HSAs)
    as health goal, v
    methods to achieve, 166
wellness programs, employer-
    sponsored, 148–149
wellness training, 167
Wheel of Retailing, 102–103
work/life balance, 94–96
working conditions in hospitals,
    87–89
Worthington Industries,
    148–149

Y
Young, Brigham, 142